The Indiana
Book of Quotes

The Indiana
Book of Quotes

Fred D. Cavinder

Indiana Historical Society Press
Indianapolis 2005

Printed in the United States of America

This book is a publication of the
Indiana Historical Society Press
450 West Ohio Street
Indianapolis, Indiana 46202-3269 USA
www.indianahistory.org

Telephone orders 1-800-447-1830
Fax orders 317-234-0562
Orders by e-mail shop.indianahistory.org

The paper in this publication meets the minimum requirements of American National Standard for Information Sciences—Permanence of Paper for Printed Library Materials, ANSI Z39.48-1984. ∞

Library of Congress Cataloging-in-Publication Data

The Indiana book of quotes / [compiled by] Fred D. Cavinder.
    p. cm.
  Includes index.
  ISBN 0-87195-183-5 (pbk. : alk. paper)
  1. Quotations, American--Indiana. I. Cavinder, Fred D., 1931- II. Title.

PN6081.I45 2005
081'.09772--dc22

                                                        2005049234

*Dedicated to the many Hoosiers
and adopted Hoosiers whose comments
and written statements through
the years have been worth repeating.*

Contents

Quotation Categories

Introduction

The king of quotations, at least in the sports field, would have to be Yogi Berra, the Yankee catcher, whose malapropisms were legendary. But Berra knew what he was saying when he was quoted as saying, "I didn't say all the things I said." He knew in his own way that quotations, once assigned to a person, whether rightly or wrongly, seem to remain forever affixed.

Hoosiers have suffered a similar fate. It was, some believe, John B. L. Soule, editor of the *Terre Haute Express*, who wrote in an editorial his advice of "Go West, young man and grow up with the country." But when New York editor Horace Greeley wrote that he agreed with Soule, the public perception was that Greeley had originated the statement. Why not? Greeley was famous (he once ran for United States president). Soule, a national nobody, failed to get credit. Soule, it was said, was inspired to write his editorial by former Indiana congressman Richard Thompson, who had just been to the West and saw its potential. Thompson also suffered a minor misapplication; when a statue of Thompson was erected on the courthouse lawn in Terre Haute, it faced east.

A different sort of quotation problem resulted when Neil Armstrong, an adopted Hoosier because he studied at Purdue University, landed on the moon in 1969. Armstrong had intended to say "That's a small step for a man, one giant leap for mankind," but it came out "That's one small step for man, one giant leap for mankind," leaving out the "a." Armstrong's fluff of the line did not make much sense, but it was too late. Even though the space agency tried to set it right, history records Armstrong's misstatement.

Some quotations, although startling, have never gained fame for various reasons, and justifiably so. Albert H. Losche, who was mayor of Indianapolis for a while (appointed when the previous mayor resigned), was wont to wax nostalgic at times. Reporters swore he sometimes prefaced his remarks with, "I never will remember." This puzzling syntax never reached the newspaper pages, however.

Those more famous than Losche got better press, in a way. Casey Stengel, the baseball manager who mouthed almost as many brain twisters as Berra, sometimes was rephrased by the press. When he asked one day, "Can't anybody play this here game?" the reporters manipulated his syntax to say "Can't anybody here play this game?" The corrected version is what is remembered.

Some things are not exactly quoted, but reference to them is as damaging as the statements themselves. Earl Butz, secretary of agriculture, with a distinguished career at Purdue University, was driven out of that office by what he said, but one seldom saw what he said in print. It can be found somewhere in archives perhaps, but usually is referred to as a bawdy racial reference. What Butz did was tell a joke about African Americans, which was far from politically correct. It was the kind of thing men tell all the time around the watercooler, but do not look for it in books of quotations.

Although Butz never said he was misquoted, others have objected to words put in their mouths. Willie Sutton denied ever saying he robbed banks because "That's where the money is." It just showed up one day in print and has hung on forever. So maybe Hoosier Jimmy Hoffa never said, "Always run from a knife and rush a gun," but that's what is remembered.

So these quotations are gleaned from all kinds of sources. Maybe they are inaccurate, the result of some reporter mishearing something or (can you believe it?) making up a good quote to fill out copy and add luster to a personality. Nevertheless, this is how people remember, or claim to remember, what they have heard Hoosiers say over the years.

Some of the Hoosiers quoted in this volume have only a passing acquaintance with Indiana. Ambrose Bierce was not a native Hoosier, but he grew up in the state. He left the state and never came back. Bierce, a noted pundit, has so many quotations to his credit that to quote them all would constitute a book in itself. In fact, there are such books, most notably Bierce's *The Devil's Dictionary*. Edgar Watson Howe only spent a short time after his birth in Indiana, but at one time, now forgotten, he was one of the nation's top pundits as an author and newspaper editor in Kansas. Frank McKinney (Kin) Hubbard, pundit with the *Indianapolis News*, created so many sayings uttered through the fictional mouth of Abe Martin that they constitute a book-length collection.

Some may question if some of those quoted are Hoosiers, as in the case of Abraham Lincoln. He may belong to the ages, but he spent his impressionable youth in Indiana. Also, the three schoolmasters who gave Lincoln his only formal education did so in Indiana. It would seem, then, that Lincoln's noted quotations, many of them uttered during his presidency, qualify him for inclusion in a Hoosier volume.

This book makes no claim to include neither every Hoosier nor near Hoosier whose pithy comments have ever been recorded, nor, of those quoted, such as Hubbard, to extract the definitive kernels of their declarations. Also included are some who are not Hoosiers in the traditional sense, but who have such a linkage with Indiana, or have spent such significant time in the state that they are

Hoosiers by adoption. Henry Ward Beecher, for example, has little connection to Indiana except that he started his ministry with churches in Lawrenceburg and Indianapolis. But this faint link with Hoosierland is enough to include many of his quotable sayings in this work. Of course, there is a tendency to attach an Indiana tag to many with only a nodding acquaintanceship with the state. An Indiana newspaperman once noted that anybody who has passed over or through the state by rail, car, or airplane is tagged with the Hoosier label.

There have been enough Hoosiers of celebrity status, for one reason or another, to provide a broad spectrum of the quotes. When you add the Hoosiers who may be little known outside the state, but who have shown glibness within Indiana, there are plenty of words of wit and worthiness. If only Yogi Berra had been a Hoosier.

Quotations by Hoosiers

Ability

Ability: That which distinguishes able men from dead men.

Ambrose Bierce

As a preacher he [Henry Ward Beecher] is a landscape painter of Christianity.

Bierce

In the last analysis, ability is commonly found to consist mainly in a high degree of solemnity.

Bierce

Ambidextrous: Able to pick with equal skill a right-hand pocket or a left.

Bierce

I am like the fellow who identified twenty-eight flavors of liquor and he identified them correctly and then they gave him water and he said: "I don't know what it is, but you can't sell it."

Lewis B. Hershey

I don't think you could lead a whore to bed.

Robert Montgomery (Bobby) Knight
to player Steve Alford

Accident

Accident: An inevitable occurrence due to the action of immutable natural laws.

Ambrose Bierce

Adversity

Affliction comes to us all not to make us sad, but sober, not to make us sorry, but wise, not to make us despondent, but by its darkness to refresh us, as the night refreshes the day; not to impoverish but to enrich us, as the plow enriches the field; to multiply our joy, as the seed, by planting, is multiplied a thousandfold.

Henry Ward Beecher

The world's battlefields have been in the heart chiefly; more heroism has been displayed in the household and the closet, than on the memorable battlefields in history.

Beecher

Half the spiritual difficulties that men and women suffer arise from a morbid state of health.

Beecher

Difficulties are God's errands; and when we are sent upon them we should esteem it a proof of God's confidences—as a compliment from him.

Beecher

A helping word to one in trouble is often like a switch on a railroad track—an inch between wreck and smooth-rolling prosperity.

Beecher

You have come into a hard world. I know of only one easy place in it, and that is the grave.

Beecher

Calamity: A more than commonly plain and unmistakable reminder that the affairs of this life are not of our own ordering. Calamities are of two kinds; misfortune to ourselves, and good fortune to others.

Ambrose Bierce

Distress: A disease incurred by exposure to the prosperity of a friend.

Bierce

Misfortune: The kind of fortune that never misses.

Bierce

No man can smile in the face of adversity and mean it.

Edgar W. Howe

As a man handles his troubles during the day, he goes to bed at night a general, captain, or private.

Howe

Your heart leads you into scrapes from which your head has to extricate you.

Howe

I'd say this for adversity: people seem able to stand it, and that's more than I can say for prosperity.

Frank McKinney (Kin) Hubbard

The fiery trials through which we pass will light us down in honor or dishonor to the last generation. —Abraham Lincoln

There is no sense in the struggle, but there is no choice but to struggle.

Ernie Pyle

Remember, you are not handicapped so long as you can think logically. You will be handicapped only if you are sloven in your thinking.

Ralph R. Teetor
blind industrialist

Suffering is also one of the ways of knowing you're alive.

Jessamyn West

In no direction that we turn do we find ease or comfort. If we are honest and if we have the will to win we find only danger, hard work, and iron resolution.

Wendell L. Willkie

Advertising

The advertisements in a newspaper are more full of knowledge in respect to what is going on in a state or community than the editorial columns are.

Henry Ward Beecher

If nature won't, Pluto will.

Advertising claim of Pluto laxative

If Pluto won't, make your will.

Rejoinder to Pluto's claim

Doing business without advertising is like winking at a girl in the dark; you know what you are doing but nobody else does.

Edgar W. Howe

Even merit has to be advertised before it pays.

Frank McKinney (Kin) Hubbard

You don't have to peddle a good thing.

Hubbard

What kills a skunk is the publicity it gives itself.

Abraham Lincoln

Early to bed, early to rise, work like hell and advertise.

William Scholl
attributed as his credo

What passes for culture in my head is really a bunch of commercials.

Kurt Vonnegut

Advice

Early to bed and early to rise, and you'll meet very few of our best people.

George Ade

In uplifting, get underneath.

Ade

Do unto yourself as your neighbors do unto themselves and look pleasant.

Ade

Advice to unwilling men is like hailstones on slate roofs; it strikes and rattles and rolls down and does them no good.

Henry Ward Beecher

It is not well for a man to pray cream and live skim milk.

Beecher

We are a conquering race. We must obey our blood and occupy new markets and if necessary new lands.

Albert J. Beveridge

Advice: The smallest current coin.

Ambrose Bierce

Consult: To seek another's advice on a course already decided upon.

Bierce

Advice: The suggestions you give someone else that you hope will work for your benefit.

Bierce

You can't scare a man about falling out of bed when he's already asleep on the floor.

Roger Branigin

Aim high. You can always hit something low down.

Bruce Calvert

The first and great commandment is, don't let them scare you.

Elmer Davis

In soloing—as in other activities—it is far easier to start something than it is to finish it.

Amelia Earhart

A man reaches the zenith at forty, the top of the hill. From that time forward he begins to descend. If you have any great undertaking ahead, begin it now. You will never be so capable again.

John Milton Hay

Electric fans should be sharpened every season.

Don Herold

If today's average American is confronted with an hour of leisure, he is likely to palpitate with panic. An hour with nothing to do! So he jumps into a dither and into a car, and starts driving off fiercely in pursuit of diversion. . . . I thank heaven I grew up in a small town, in a horse-and-buggy era, when we had, or made, time to sit and think, and often just to sit. . . . We need less leg action and more acute observation as we go. Slow down the muscles and stir up the mind.

Herold

Always run from a knife and rush a gun.

Jimmy Hoffa

A good scare is worth more to a man than good advice.

Edgar W. Howe

Remember this: a man doesn't have to look the part.

Howe

Abuse a man unjustly, and you will make friends for him.

Howe

There is some advice that is too good—the advice to love your enemy, for instance.

Howe

If you want to save money, don't eat anything: this advice is impractical, but so is most good advice.

Howe

You won't skid if you stay in a rut.

Frank McKinney (Kin) Hubbard

The early tire gets the roofing tack.

Hubbard

Look out for the fellow who lets you do all the talking.

Hubbard

If you want to get rid of somebody just tell them something for their own good.

Hubbard

The worst waste of breath, next to playing a saxophone, is advising a son.

Hubbard

A never-failing way to get rid of a fellow is to tell him something for his own good.

Hubbard

It is best not to swap horses while crossing the river. —Abraham Lincoln

When you have got an elephant by the hind leg, and he is trying to run away, it's best to let him run.

Lincoln

You can't escape the responsibility of tomorrow by evading it today.

Lincoln

Go west, young man, go west!

John L. B. Soule
attributed

If you can't lick them, join them.

James E. Watson
attributed, among others

My first maxim is, be lucky.

Herman B Wells

Age

We have grown some ivy, but we have not yet taken on moss.

George Ade

A man in old age is like a sword in a shop window.

Henry Ward Beecher

From childhood to youth is eternity; from youth to manhood, a season. Age comes in a night and is incredible.

Ambrose Bierce

Age: That period of life in which we compound for the vices that remain by reviling those we have no longer the vigor to commit.

Bierce

Young gorillas are friendly, but they soon learn.

William Jacob Cuppy

When a middle-age man says in a moment of weariness that he is half dead, he is telling the literal truth.

Elmer Davis

I never tell anyone my age. I was thirty-nine last year and this year I'm thirty-eight—and if I live long enough I'll be an infant when I die.

Jane (Mrs. Carl) Fisher

At my age, I don't even buy green bananas.

Phil Harris at age 84

The Union soldiers and sailors are now veterans of time as well as war. The parallels of age have approached close to the citadels of life and the end, for each, of a brave and honorable struggle is not remote.

Benjamin Harrison

It is but a few short years from diapers to dignity and from dignity to decomposition.

Don Herold

A boy becomes an adult three years before his parents think he does, and about two years after he thinks he does.

Lewis B. Hershey

Age alone is no real guarantee of quality unless one is considering red wine or cheese.

Theodore Hesburgh

If you want to know how old a woman is, ask her sister-in-law.

Edgar W. Howe

After a woman reaches fifty, she is usually called upon to deny her weight as well as her age.

Howe

After a man passes sixty, his mischief is mainly in his head.

Howe

A woman is as old as she looks before breakfast.

Howe

As you grow older gradually accustom yourself to neglect.

Howe

The only thing some people do is to grow older.

Howe

Men get old before they know it, but women don't.

Frank McKinney (Kin) Hubbard

Why is it that the first gray hairs stick straight out?

Hubbard

You've got to be fifty-nine years old to believe a fellow is at his best at sixty.

Hubbard

When a fellow begins to complain of the immodesty of women, he's getting pretty well along in years.

Hubbard

An old-timer is a fellow who remembers when, if a woman had to be carried out of a place, she had either fainted or died.

Hubbard

You know how to tell when you're getting old? When your broad mind changes places with your narrow waist.

Red Skelton

Maturity is a bitter disappointment for which no remedy exists, unless laughter can be said to remedy anything.

Kurt Vonnegut

Agriculture

When I was a small boy being on a farm the year round was a good deal like being in jail, except that the prisoners who were in jail were not required to work fourteen hours a day. . . . The good old days were not so good, and the nights were much worse.

George Ade

About the only thing on a farm that has an easy time is the dog.

Edgar W. Howe

Even if a farmer intends to loaf, he gets up in time to get an early start.

Howe

One good thing about living on a farm is that you can fight with your wife without being heard.

Frank McKinney (Kin) Hubbard

Farming looks nice—from a car window.

Hubbard

I don't think I could have played the part if I hadn't lived on a farm in Indiana.

Marjorie Main
on her role as Ma Kettle

I don't need to study scripts to play my screen roles. All I need to do is remember the warm-hearted, generous, fun-loving, honest, sincere, down-to-earth Hoosiers.

Main

Ambition

She invariably was first over the fence in the mad pursuit of culture.

George Ade

Ambition: An overmastering desire to be vilified by enemies while living and made ridiculous by friends when dead.

Ambrose Bierce

Amateur: A public nuisance who confounds his ambition with his ability.

Bierce

Every nation has a prominent citizen who builds a pyramid.

Edgar W. Howe

A loafer always has the correct time.

Frank McKinney (Kin) Hubbard

Every man is said to have his peculiar ambition. I have no other so great as that of being truly esteemed by my fellow man, by rendering myself worthy of their esteem.

Abraham Lincoln

Ancestry

Genealogy: An account of one's descent from an ancestor who did not particularly care to trace his own.

Ambrose Bierce

Ancestry: The known part of the route from an arboreal ancestor with a swim bladder to an urban descendant with a cigarette.

Bierce

Ancestry is a good thing. Few people can get along without it. It seems to be an absolute household necessity.

Thomas R. Marshall

Anger

Always select the right sort of parents before you start to be rough.

George Ade

A man that does not know how to be angry does not know how to be good.

Henry Ward Beecher

Never forget what a man says to you when he is angry.

Beecher

Speak when you are angry and you will make the best speech you will ever regret.

Ambrose Bierce

Rant: High-sounding language unsupported by dignity of thought.

Bierce

Don't ever slam a door; you might want to go back.

Don Herold

People always say that they are not themselves when tempted by anger into betraying what they really are.

Edgar W. Howe

If you want to make a man very angry, get someone to pray for him.

Howe

It seems to make an auto driver mad if he misses you.

Frank McKinney (Kin) Hubbard

Too many of us become enraged because we have to bear the shortcomings of others. We should remember that not one of us is perfect, and that others see our defects as obviously as we see theirs. . . . Let us, therefore, bear the shortcomings of each other for the ultimate benefit of everyone.

Abraham Lincoln

No man can think clearly when his fists are clenched.

George Jean Nathan

Animals

God forbid that I should build a fire for my comfort that should be the means of destroying one of His creatures.

Johnny Appleseed
on seeing a mosquito die in his campfire

The dog was created especially for children. He is the god of frolic.

Henry Ward Beecher

The monkey is an organized sarcasm upon the human race.

Beecher

Dog: The only popular tail bearer.

Ambrose Bierce

Dog: A kind of additional or subsidiary deity designed to catch the overflow and surplus of the world's worship.

Bierce

Mouse: An animal which strews its path with fainting women.

Bierce

Cat: A soft, indestructible automaton provided by nature to be kicked when things go wrong in the domestic circle.

Bierce

Rattlesnake: Our prostrate brother.

Bierce

Monkey: An arboreal animal that makes itself at home in genealogical trees.

Bierce

If an animal does something, we call it instinct; if we do the same thing for the same reason, we call it intelligence.

William Jacob Cuppy

What really happened to the buffalos is just what you might expect if you've ever seen one in a zoo—the moths got into them.

Cuppy

Frogs will eat red-flannel worms fed to them by biologists; this proves a great deal about both parties concerned.

Cuppy

The beaver is very industrious, but he is still a beaver. —*Cuppy*

Some people lose all respect for the lion unless he devours them instantly. There is no pleasing some people.

Cuppy

Becoming extinct is the perfect answer to everything, and I defy anybody to think of a better one.

Cuppy

The dodo seems to have been invented for the sole purpose of becoming extinct, and that was all he was good for.

Cuppy

The hippopotamus looks monogamous—he looks as if he would have to be.

Cuppy

A stockman should never rest until the air in his stable in winter is inoffensive.

E. Chubb Fuller

THE INDIANA BOOK OF QUOTES

Man is the only animal that plays poker.

Don Herold

The most comfortable people on a hayride are the horses.

Herold

The meanest family I know has rabbit for Easter dinner.

Herold

The way to keep a cat is to try to chase it away.

Edgar W. Howe

No matter how much cats fight, there always seem to be plenty of kittens.

Abraham Lincoln

It just proves that fifty million Frenchmen can't be wrong. They eat horses instead of ride them.

Cole Porter
after his fall from a horse in 1937

Annoyance

The feeling of sleepiness when you are not in bed, and can't get there, is the meanest feeling in the world.

Edgar W. Howe

Nothing is as mean as giving a little child something useful for Christmas.

Frank McKinney (Kin) Hubbard

Appearance

The plain people are worth dying for until you bunch them and give them the cold once-over, and then they impress the impartial observer as being slightly bovine, with a large percentage of vegetable tissue.

George Ade

Clothes and manners do not make the man; but, when he is made, they greatly improve his appearance.

Henry Ward Beecher

Ugliness: A gift of the gods to certain women, entailing virtue without humility.

Ambrose Bierce

Self-evident: Evident to one's self and to nobody else.

Bierce

Beard: The hair that is commonly cut off by those who justly execrate the absurd Chinese custom of shaving the head.

Bierce

It's easy to see the faults in people I know; it's hardest to see the good, especially when the good isn't there.

William Jacob Cuppy

There's one thing about baldness: it's neat.

Don Herold

Dark circles under the eyes are not made with a compass.

Herold

When the men meet a bride, they look at her face; the women look at her clothes.

Edgar W. Howe

A man is usually bald four or five years before he knows it.

Howe

After a man is fifty, you can fool him by saying he is smart, but you can't fool him by saying he is handsome.

Howe

When a woman dresses in a hurry, she always looks it.

Howe

He had the widest, blackest and best-groomed and longest beard I've ever seen off a yak.

Frank McKinney (Kin) Hubbard

False teeth are all right in their place.

Hubbard

Young Lafe Bud says he always hates to get his hair cut because it makes his hat look so old.

Hubbard

Some folks, like most restaurants, seem to think a clean front is all that's necessary.

Hubbard

Some folks look so busy doing nothing that they seem indispensable.

Hubbard

If I had two faces, would I be wearing this one?

Abraham Lincoln
when accused of being two-faced

Common-looking people are the best in the world: that is the reason the Lord made so many of them.

Lincoln

Every man over forty is responsible for his face.

Lincoln

As to whiskers, having never worn any, do you not think people would call it a piece of silly affectation if I were to begin it now?

Lincoln

Applause

Applause is the echo of a platitude.

Ambrose Bierce

Nobody kicks on being interrupted if it's by applause.

Frank McKinney (Kin) Hubbard

Another style of four-flushing is applauding an imitation of an actor you never saw.

Hubbard

Applause is nothing compared with laughter. Anyone can clap hands, and the mind be miles away. A laugh comes right from the center. No wonder comedians love their audiences.

Jessamyn West

Argument

Discussion: A method of confirming others in their errors.

Ambrose Bierce

Controversy: A battle in which spittle or ink replaces the injurious cannonball and the inconsiderate bayonet.

Bierce

Positive: Being mistaken at the top of one's voice.

Bierce

There are two sides to the story when men quarrel, but at least a dozen when women quarrel.

Edgar W. Howe

The sounder your argument, the more satisfaction you get out of it.

Howe

You can make up a quarrel, but it will always show where it was patched.

Howe

You may easily plan a joke on a man who likes to argue—agree with him.

Howe

The best way to win an argument is to begin by being right.

Jill Ruckelshaus

Arts

Every artist dips his brush in his own soul and paints his own nature into his pictures.

Henry Ward Beecher

Painting: The art of protecting flat surfaces from the weather and exposing them to critics.

Ambrose Bierce

Realism: The art of depicting nature as it is seen by toads.

Bierce

Dance: To leap about to the sounds of tittering music, preferably with arms about your neighbor's wife or daughter.

Bierce

Art: This word has no definition.

Bierce

Art is the stored honey of the human soul, gathered on the wings of misery and travail.

Theodore Dreiser

Actresses will happen even in the best of families.

Don Herold

Carefulness is the laziest form of art.

Herold

What is worse than having someone try to tell you about a play they saw?

Frank McKinney (Kin) Hubbard

Pop is either hard-core or hard-edge.

Robert Indiana

I am not sure acting is a thing for a grown man.

Steve McQueen

All art is a kind of subconscious madness expressed in terms of sanity.

George Jean Nathan

Hollywood, so far as any art goes, is like having an exciting affair with a very rich and very ambitious eunuch.

Nathan

Art is reaching out into the ugliness of the world for vagrant beauty and the imprisoning of it in a tangible dream.

Nathan

Great art is as irrational as great music. It is mad with its own loveliness.

Nathan

To speak of morals in art is to speak of legislature in sex. Art is the sex of the imagination.

Nathan

Art is the gross exaggeration of natural beauty.

Nathan

An artist never strikes; he leaves such things to plumbers and street sweepers.

Nathan

In the theater a hero is one who believes that all women are ladies; a villain, one who believes that all ladies are women.

Nathan

A ham is simply an actor who has not been successful in repressing his natural instincts.

Nathan

Opening night is the night before the play is ready to open.

Nathan

Actors are men who sleep till noon and spend the afternoon calling on women.

Nathan

Speaking of art—I know a fellow over at Terre Haute that can spit clean over a box car.

James Whitcomb Riley
after hearing a lecture
on art at John Herron Art
Institute in Indianapolis

Revolutions aren't good for art. Gentle artists die, or vanish; the other kind tend to become propagandists.

Booth Tarkington

Dancing is like bank robbery, it takes split-second timing.

Twyla Tharp

I have the canary-bird-in-the-coal-mine theory of the arts; artists should be treasured as alarm systems.

Kurt Vonnegut

My God, did I set all this in motion?

Lew Wallace
on seeing Ben-Hur *staged*

Attitude

Familiarity breeds contentment.

George Ade

The prouder a man is, the more he thinks he deserves; and the more he thinks he deserves, the less he really deserves.

Henry Ward Beecher

Nothing dies so hard, or rallies so often, as intolerance.

Beecher

Zeal: A certain nervous disorder afflicting the young and inexperienced.

Ambrose Bierce

Impartial: Unable to perceive any promise of personal advantage from espousing either side of a controversy.

Bierce

Neighbor: One whom we are commanded to love as ourselves, and does all he knows how to make us disobedient.

Bierce

Resolute: Obstinate in a course that we approve.

Bierce

Ingrate: One who receives a benefit from another, or is otherwise an object of charity.

Bierce

Reverence: The spiritual attitude of a man to a god and a dog to man.

Bierce

Vulgarity, if it be boisterous enough, often passes for fame.

Max Ehrmann

A lot of men think that if they smile for a second, somebody will take advantage of them, and they are right.

Don Herold

We used to be good friends of the Blanks, but we out-bla-sed them.

Herold

When a man is trying to sell you something, don't imagine that he is that polite all the time.

Howe

The man who is said to have his heart in the right place is apt to have something wrong with his head.

Howe

Nothing tires a man more than to be grateful all the time.

Howe

One of the surprising things of this world is the respect a worthless man has for himself.

Howe

It would be a swell world if everybody was as pleasant as the fellow who's trying to skin you.

Frank McKinney (Kin) Hubbard

The fellow that's pleased with everything either doesn't cut any ice or has something up his sleeve.

Hubbard

The fellow that says "I may be wrong, but—" does not believe there can be any such possibility.

Hubbard

When small things upset someone my grandmother used to say, "Nonsense! That would never be noticed from a trotting horse."

Emily Kimbrough

I guess maybe people are attracted to a no-bullshit guy who tells people to shove it up their ass when he thinks it's appropriate.

Robert Montgomery (Bobby) Knight

The great problems of the world—social, political, economic and theological— do not concern me in the slightest. . . . If all the Armenians were to be killed tomorrow and if half of Russia were to starve to death the day after, it would not matter to me in the least. What concerns me alone is myself and the interest of a few close friends.

George Jean Nathan

With attitude you can just about get anybody through anything.

William J. Schroeder

No man has a right in America to treat any other man tolerantly, for tolerance is the assumption of superiority. Our liberties are equal rights of every citizen.

Wendell L. Willkie

Autos

Frankly, I did not realize on that Fourth of July, when I took the first ride in America's first car, that a score of years later every street and highway in America would echo the sound of the horn and the report of the exhaust.

Elwood Haynes

You won't meet any autos in the straight-and-narrow path. —Frank McKinney (Kin) Hubbard

Aviation

I cruised inland until I found a suitable pasture. I landed there after frightening all the cows in the neighborhood and rolled up to a farmer's front door.

Amelia Earhart

Of course I realized there was a measure of danger. Obviously I faced the possibility of not returning when first I considered going. Once faced and settled there really wasn't any good reason to refer to it.

Earhart
on her flight
in the Friendship

I have a feeling that there is just about one more good flight left in my system, and I hope this is it.

Earhart
before her fatal flight

Flying might not be all plain sailing, but the fun of it is worth the price.

Earhart

I believe that I could have turned and circled the track but Mr. Curtiss has absolutely forbidden me attempting the turns until I have mastered straight flights.

Blanche Stuart Scott
after the first flight by a female
at Fort Wayne, 1910

I took an economy flight. There wasn't any movie, but they flew low over drive-ins.

Red Skelton

The boys have flown.

Milton Wright
on hearing his sons had
succeeded at Kitty Hawk

When my brother and I built and flew the first man-carrying flying machine, we thought that we were introducing into the world an invention that would make further wars practically impossible, . . . We thought governments would realize the impossibility of winning by surprise attacks, and that no country would enter into war with another when it knew it would have to win by simply wearing out the enemy.

Orville Wright

In the kingdom of the birds, the parrot is the best talker—and the worst flier.

Orville Wright

Man won't be flying for a thousand years.

Wilbur Wright,
two years before Kitty Hawk

I can't afford to support a wife and a flying machine too.

Wilbur Wright

It is possible to fly without motors, but not without knowledge and skill.

Wilbur Wright

Four flights Thursday morning. All against twenty-one-mile wind. Started from level with engine power alone. Average speed through air thirty-one miles. Longest fifty-nine seconds. Inform press. Home Christmas.

Orville and Wilbur Wright
telegram to their father

Beauty

She was short on intellect, but long on shape.

George Ade

Her features did not seem to know the value of teamwork.

Ade

The creator and arbiter of beauty is the heart; to the male rattlesnake the female rattlesnake is the loveliest thing in nature.

Ambrose Bierce

Beauty: The power by which a woman charms a lover and terrifies a husband.

Bierce

A woman with any sort of figure is prouder of it than a man is of a million dollars.

Edgar W. Howe

Beauty is only skin deep, but it's a valuable asset if you're poor and haven't any sense.

Frank McKinney (Kin) Hubbard

We now have 7,000 beauty preparations, or about 289 for each beauty.

Hubbard

If you haven't seen your wife smile at a traffic cop, you haven't seen her smile her prettiest.

Hubbard

Beauty makes idiots sad and wise men merry.

George Jean Nathan

Back home we had a beauty contest once and nobody won.

Herb Shriner

Beauty is altogether in the eye of the beholder.

Lew Wallace
in The Prince of India

The tragedy of our time is that we are so eye centered, so appearance besotted.

Jessamyn West

Behavior

Next to ingratitude, the most painful thing to bear is gratitude.

Henry Ward Beecher

Every charitable act is a stepping stone toward heaven.

Beecher

To apologize is to lay the foundation for a future offense.

Ambrose Bierce

Apostate: A leech who, having penetrated the shell of a turtle only to find that the creature has long been dead, deems it expedient to form a new attachment to a fresh turtle.

Bierce

Alone: In bad company.

Bierce

Take: To acquire, frequently by force but preferably by stealth.

Bierce

Gratitude: A sentiment lying midway between a benefit received and a benefit expected.

Bierce

The gods love a cheerful grumbler.

Bruce Calvert

Just when you're beginning to think pretty well of people, you run across somebody who puts sugar on sliced tomatoes.

William Jacob Cuppy

Be good, even at the cost of your self-respect.

Don Herold

Be kind and considerate to others, depending somewhat upon who they are.

Herold

Be kind to dumb people.

Herold

I do unto others what they do unto me, only worse.

Jimmy Hoffa

If a loafer is not a nuisance to you, it is a sign that you are somewhat of a loafer yourself.

Edgar W. Howe

The way out of trouble is never as simple as the way in. —Howe

When you are in trouble, people who call to sympathize are really looking for the particulars.

Howe

We are all pretty much alike when we get out of town.

Frank McKinney (Kin) Hubbard

Lack of pep is often mistaken for patience.

Hubbard

It's pretty hard to be efficient without being obnoxious.

Hubbard

He has ever been the tin can on his own tail.

George Jean Nathan

I have spent my life escaping boredom, not because I am bored, but because I do not want to be.

Cole Porter

Living in a small town is peaceful. You don't do much. You're afraid to. You're sure to get caught.

Herb Shriner

Laughter or crying is what a human being does when there's nothing else he can do.

Kurt Vonnegut

As a rule, there is no surer way to the dislike of men than to behave well where they have behaved badly.

Lew Wallace

Beliefs

Absurdity: A statement or belief manifestly inconsistent with one's own opinion.
Ambrose Bierce

Force is all-conquering, but its victories are short-lived.
Abraham Lincoln

Superstition is the belief that all stage kisses give no satisfaction to the actor or actresses.

George Jean Nathan

Birds

Robins are the most indulgent parents of all birds. I've seen a mother robin lead a youngster right up to a worm and point it out, but in spite of all she can do, she finally had to pick it up for the youngster and hand it to him. Young robins will not work till they just have to.

Frank McKinney (Kin) Hubbard

Books

Only the more rugged mortals should attempt to keep up with current literature.

George Ade

Where is human nature so weak as in the bookstore?

Henry Ward Beecher

A book is a garden, an orchard, a storehouse, a party, a company by the way, a counselor, a multitude of counselors.

Beecher

Books are not made for furniture but there is nothing else that so beautifully furnishes a house.

Beecher

A library is but the soul's burial ground. It is the land of shadows.

Beecher

Book: A malevolent literary device for cramping the growth of the language and making it hard and inelastic.

Ambrose Bierce

Publish: In literary affairs, to become the fundamental element in a core of critics.

Bierce

The covers of this book are too far apart.

Bierce

Novel: A short story padded. A species of composition bearing the same relation to literature that the panorama bears to art.

Bierce

Sartor Resartus is simply unreadable, and for me that always sort of spoils a book.

William Jacob Cuppy

The trouble with the dictionary is that you have to know how a word is spelled before you can look it up to see how it is spelled.

Cuppy

The masses are reading for the first time in history. Externals are mistaken for internals, clothes for brains, loud talk for strength of character, cheap wit for intelligence.

Max Ehrmann

Every little while another man decides what are the best books. Pay no attention to him and decide for yourself.

Edgar W. Howe

Reading is like permitting a man to talk a long time and refusing you the right to answer.

Howe

Anybody that's got time to read half of the new books has got entirely too much time.

Frank McKinney (Kin) Hubbard

Everything comes to him who waits but a loaned book.

Hubbard

No fellow ought to publish a book unless he's got a trade to fall back on.

Hubbard

People who like this sort of thing will find this the sort of thing they like.
Abraham Lincoln
assessing a book

Books serve to show a man that those original thoughts of his aren't very new at all.
Lincoln

The longtime librarian of Purdue University, John Moriarity, examined the authorship of the ten best-selling novels each year from 1900 to 1940. By allowing ten points for the number-one best-seller, nine points for the second best, and so on, down to one point for the tenth book on the list, he totaled up a score of 213 points for Indiana authors in that long period. That score was exceeded only slightly by New York's 218 points.

Howard H. Peckham

My theory is that people who don't like detective stories are anarchists.

Rex Stout

If you want to know me, my books are the best way, for . . . they furnish a better biography than I can write.

Gene Stratton-Porter

To my way of thinking and working, the greatest service a piece of fiction can do any reader is to force him to lay it down with a higher ideal of life than he had when he took it up.

Stratton-Porter

If I had a hundred years to live and strength to write a book for every one of them I could fill them all cram full of comparatively new, interesting things, from everyday life about me.

Stratton-Porter

Science fiction: Comic books—without pictures. —Kurt Vonnegut

I have been a sorehead occupant of a file drawer labeled "Science Fiction" . . . and I would like out, particularly since so many serious critics regularly mistake the drawer for a urinal.

Vonnegut

The British

It must be a comfort to the English to know the guard is going to be changed three times a day whether it needs it or not.

Don Herold

The chief occupation of the English is intonation.

Herold

Business

No matter who reigns, the merchant reigns.

Henry Ward Beecher

Every young man would do well to remember that all successful business stands on the foundation of morality.

Beecher

The gambling known as business looks with austere disfavor upon the business known as gambling.

Ambrose Bierce

Freebooter: A conqueror in a small way of business whose annexations lack the sanctifying merit of magnitude.

Bierce

Corporation: An ingenious device for obtaining individual profit without individual responsibility.

Bierce

Insurance: An ingenious modern game of chance in which the player is permitted to enjoy the comfortable conviction that he is beating the man who keeps the table.

Bierce

We hear a good deal about business confidence, which means confidence of business in itself, in its government, and in its capacity for expansion. But confidence is only another way of saying that people believe each other, keep their promises, pay their debts, and regard their duty to society. As long as business observes these rules, it will have the confidence of the community and it will be safe from all of the irresponsible attacks of its enemies.

Will H. Hays

Half the time when men think they are talking business, they are wasting time.

Edgar W. Howe

Make your business talks as short as your prayers and you will always be a winner.

Howe

No man knows where his business ends and his neighbor's begins.

Howe

In thousands of years there has been no advance in public morals, in philosophy, in religion, or in politics, but the advance in business has been the greatest miracle the world has ever known.

Howe

Every great improvement in the world's history is due, directly or indirectly, to the munificence of some man successful in the world's affairs. Every great charitable institution is founded on the surplus earnings of active men who did good while earning the money and, having learned philanthropy, closed their lives with a burst of it. The men of great learning did not build the institutions in which they teach, although nearly all of them unjustly criticize the men who did.

Howe

A fellow who knows his business is always reticent.

Frank McKinney (Kin) Hubbard

If the government was as afraid of disturbing the consumer as it is of disturbing business, this would be some democracy.

Hubbard

When I was a kid, I remember how my grandfather used to trim the window in his little store. All he did was to wash the cat and put in some clean flypaper.

Herb Shriner

The glory of the United States is business.

Wendell L. Willkie

Challenges

The hardest thing is to take less when you can get more.

Frank McKinney (Kin) Hubbard

The occasion is piled high with difficulty, and we must rise high with the occasion.

Abraham Lincoln

Now, gentlemen, we have got our harpoon into the monster, but we must still take uncommon care, or else by a single flop of his tail he will send us all to eternity.

Lincoln

Character

A man's reputation is the reality of himself. His reputation is the opinion others have formed of him. Character is in him; reputation is from other people—that is the substance, this is the shadow.

Henry Ward Beecher

Morality is character and conduct such as is required by the circle or community in which the man's life happens to be placed. It shows how much good men require of us.

Beecher

God appoints our graces to be nurses to other men's weakness.

Beecher

Greatness lies not in being strong, but in the right use of strength.

Beecher

Many men build as cathedrals were built, the part nearest the ground finished; but that part that soars toward heaven, the turrets and the spires, forever incomplete.

Beecher

No man is good for anything who has not some particle of obstinacy to use upon occasion.

Beecher

No man is more cheated than the selfish man.

Beecher

In each human heart are a tiger, a pig, an ass, and a nightingale; diversity of character is due to their unequal activity.

Ambrose Bierce

Hypocrite: One who, professing virtues that he does not respect, secures the advantage of seeming to be what he despises.

Bierce

Bigot: One who is obstinately and zealously attached to an opinion that you do not entertain.

Bierce

If I have one weakness, it's being myself. I never changed a damn bit whether I was in the governor's office or not.

Roger Branigin

There are three species of creatures who when they seem coming are going, and when they seem going they come: diplomats, women, and crabs.

John Milton Hay

Very few people look the part and are it too.

Don Herold

THE INDIANA BOOK OF QUOTES

Many people have character who have nothing else.

Herold

We cater to and rather encourage what you might call cussedness on the part of our local [draft] board members.

Lewis B. Hershey

I may have faults, but being wrong isn't one of them.

Jimmy Hoffa

The most natural man in a play is the villain.

Edgar W. Howe

One of the surprising things of this world is the respect a worthless man has for himself.

Howe

A fairly decent man does not need a state or national law to keep straight; his competitors and patrons usually attend to that.

Howe

A modest man is usually admired—if people ever hear of him.

Howe

I think I am better than the people who are trying to reform me.

Howe

Most attempted reforms are only publicity for the evils they would reform.

Howe

A man will do more for his stubbornness than for his religion or his country.

Howe

Most men who want to do good, want it done at the expense of others.

Howe

Doing right doesn't come as hard as getting credit for it.

Howe

The goodness of some people is the worse thing about them.

Howe

Great men are those who profit the most from the fewest mistakes.

Howe

Some folks seem to have descended from the chimpanzee much later than others.

Frank McKinney (Kin) Hubbard

The hardest thing is writing a recommendation for someone we know.

Hubbard

Honesty pays, but it doesn't seem to pay enough to suit some people.

Hubbard

Every once in a while we meet a fellow that's too proud to beg, too honest to steal, and too lazy to work.

Hubbard

A real gentleman is at a disadvantage these days.

Hubbard

A true lady or gentleman remains at home with a grouch same as if they had pneumonia.

Hubbard

Resolve to be honest at all events; and if in your judgment you cannot be an honest lawyer, resolve to be honest without being a lawyer. Choose some other occupation.

Abraham Lincoln

Nearly all men can stand adversity, but if you want to test a man's character, give him power.

Lincoln

Will springs from the two elements of moral sense and self-interest.

Lincoln

I do the very best I know how—the very best I can; and I mean to keep doing so until the end. If the end brings me out all right, what is said against me won't amount to anything. If the end brings me out wrong, ten angels swearing I was right would make no difference.

Lincoln

Character is like a tree and reputation is like its shadow. The shadow is what we think of it; the tree is the real thing.

Lincoln

Fame is a vapor, popularity an accident, and riches take wing. Only one thing endures and that is character.

Lincoln

I don't believe a man is a scoundrel just because he doesn't agree with me.

Thomas R. Marshall

The artist and the censor differ in this wise: that the first is a decent mind in an indecent body and that the second is an indecent mind in a decent body.

George Jean Nathan

I'm not a snob. I just want the best of everything.

Cole Porter

I never made a mistake in my life. —John Purdue

I made quite a name for myself back home. I left when I found out what it was.

Herb Shriner

I have always believed that I was a gentleman.

Little Turtle
upon getting gout

We are what we pretend to be so we must be careful what we pretend to be.

Kurt Vonnegut

A flaw in the human character is that everybody wants to build and nobody wants to do maintenance.

Vonnegut

A man is never so on trial as in the moment of excessive good fortune.

Lew Wallace

We can love an honest rogue, but what is more offensive than a false saint?

Jessamyn West

Be more concerned with your character than with your reputation. Your character is what you really are while your reputation is merely what others think you are.

John Wooden

Characteristics

Good humor makes all things tolerable.

Henry Ward Beecher

Aristocrats: Fellows that wear downy hats and clean shirts—guilty of education and suspected of bank accounts.

Ambrose Bierce

A man's legs must be long enough to reach the ground.

Abraham Lincoln

Suspicion and super sensitiveness are at once the badge and the bane of a little soul.

Charles Major

Children

I was sitting with a little girl of eight one afternoon. She looked up from her Hans Andersen and said, "Does m-i-r-a-g-e spell marriage, Mr. Ade?" "Yes, my child," I said.

George Ade

You cannot teach a child to take care of himself unless you will let him try to take care of himself. He will make mistakes; and out of these mistakes will come his wisdom.

Henry Ward Beecher

A baby is a mother's anchor. She cannot swing far from her moorings.

Beecher

Baby: A misshapen creature of no particular age, sex, or condition, chiefly remarkable for the violence of the sympathies and antipathies it excites in others, itself without sentiment or emotion.

Ambrose Bierce

Childhood: The period of human life intermediate between the idiocy of infancy and the folly of youth—two removes from the sin of manhood and three from the remorse of age.

Bierce

The fact that boys are allowed to exist at all is evidence of a remarkable Christian forbearance among men.

Bierce

I think that saving a little child and bringing him into his own is a darned sight better business than loafing around the throne.

John Milton Hay

This industry [the movies] must have toward that sacred thing, the mind of a child, toward that clean virgin thing, that unmarked slate, the same responsibility, the same care about impressions made upon it that the best clergyman or the most inspired teacher of youth would have.

Will H. Hays

There is little use to talk about your child to anyone; other people either have one or haven't.

Don Herold

There's no reason why any child should lack a complete knowledge of life, since there is no censorship of drugstore windows.

Herold

Babies are a very nice way to start people.

Herold

The most important thing a father can do for his children is to love their mother.

Theodore Hesburgh

Raising children is like making biscuits; it is as easy to raise a big batch as one, while you have your hands in the dough.

Edgar W. Howe

No parent was ever very comfortable with a child after it had reached twenty-five.

Howe

Don't take up a man's time talking about the smartness of your children; he wants to talk to you about the smartness of his children.

Howe

A boy doesn't have to go to war to be a hero; he can say he doesn't like pie when he sees there isn't enough to go around.

Howe

A boy's good time at a picnic begins with getting lost from his mother.

Howe

Every time a boy shows his hands, someone suggests that he wash them.

Howe

There are two ways of raising boys; judging from the men turned out both ways are wrong.

Howe

Families with babies and families without babies are sorry for each other.

Howe

After a woman has had seven children, reminiscences of her past begin to sound like statistics.

Howe

In buying presents, give a girl something she can wear and a boy something he can eat.

Howe

We like little children because they tear out as soon as they get what they want.

Frank McKinney (Kin) Hubbard

Boys will be boys and so will a lot of middle-aged men.

Hubbard

There is nothing so aggravating as a fresh boy who is too old to ignore and too young to kick.

Hubbard

What has become of all the child wonders we used to know in school?

Hubbard

The worse feature of a new baby is its mother singing.

Hubbard

About the only thing we have left that actually discriminates in favor of the plain people is the stork.

Hubbard

We never know how a son is going to turn out or when a daughter is going to turn in.

Hubbard

The reason parents no longer lead their children in the right direction is because the parents aren't going that way themselves.

Hubbard

A woman with a few children always has an alibi.

Hubbard

Every father expects his boy to do the things he wouldn't do when he was young.

Hubbard

One of the commonest mistakes is thinking your worries are over when your children get married.

Hubbard

Around home a kid would usually get his suit handed down to him from his father; then, when the kid got through with it, he'd hand it down to the next kid. In fact, if a suit had a few kids left in it, the family wouldn't throw the suit away; they'd go ahead and have the kids. It got so a woman would hate to see a good suit come into the family.

Herb Shriner

If I dood it, I gets a whipping.

Red Skelton

Any kid will run any errand for you, if you ask at bedtime.

Skelton

How can a kid ten years old find a dope pusher and the FBI can't?

Skelton

The child lives almost as much in his dreams of what will happen as the aged man does in his dreams of what has happened.

Booth Tarkington

If you want a baby, have a new one. Don't baby the old one.

Jessamyn West

I never meet anyone nowadays who admits to having had a happy childhood.

West

Cities

City life is millions of people being lonesome together.

Ambrose Bierce

You cannot stop the wicked from going to Chicago by killing them.

Bierce

Chicago is the product of modern capitalism, and, like other great commercial centers, is unfit for human habitation.

Eugene V. Debs

I have come to dread the conventional point of view. The small mind of the townsmen is anti-polar to that of the larger, more sophisticated wisdom of the city.

Theodore Dreiser

Paris is now the capital of limbo.

Janet Flanner

There is nothing distinctive about living in New York; over eight million other people are doing it.

Don Herold

New York: homes, homes everywhere, and not a place to live.

Herold

Hollywood—out where sex begins.

Herold

New York now leads the world's great cities in the number of people around whom you shouldn't make a sudden move.

David Letterman

Traffic signals in New York are just rough guidelines.

Letterman

Fall is my favorite season in Los Angeles, watching the birds change color and fall from the trees.

Letterman

I'd rather wake up in the middle of nowhere than in any city on earth.

Steve McQueen

Paris is a circus, a fair.

Joaquin Miller

Hollywood is a place where ten million dollars worth of machinery functions to put skin on baloney.

George Jean Nathan

A panic is a great teacher of humility, and the financial depression that fell upon the country in 1873 drove the lesson home remorselessly at Indianapolis. . . . The signal effect of this dark time was to stimulate thrift and bring a new era of caution and conservation; for there is a good deal of Scotch-Irish in the Hoosier, and he cannot be fooled twice with the same bait. During the period of depression the town lost its zest for gaiety.

Meredith Nicholson

To a person who has talent and is willing to work hard, Broadway in New York is as friendly as Main Street in Peru, Indiana.

—Cole Porter

Indianapolis is a big city where the meters run faster than the cabs.

Herb Shriner

I like to walk around Manhattan, catching glimpses of its wildlife, the pigeons and cats and girls.

Rex Stout

[Indianapolis] . . . where the practice of the arts was regarded as an evasion of real life by means of parlor tricks.

Kurt Vonnegut

Civilization

A savage is a man of one story, and that one story a cellar. . . . The civilized man is thirty stories deep.

Henry Ward Beecher

Intelligent discontent is the mainspring of civilization. Progress is born of agitation. It is agitation or stagnation.

Eugene V. Debs

Civilization is nothing more than politeness, industry, and fairness.

Edgar W. Howe

Civilization is teaching men to govern themselves by letting them do it.

Abraham Lincoln

Class

The germinal idea of class and group conflicts in history appeared in the writings of Aristotle, long before the Christian era. . . . It was expounded by James Madison, in No. 10 of *The Federalist*, written in defense of the Constitution of the United States, long before Karl Marx was born.

Charles A. Beard

Class and group divisions based on property lie at the basis of modern governments; and politics and constitutional law are inevitably a reflex of these contending interests.

Beard

While there is a lower class I am in it; while there is a criminal element I am of it; while there is a soul in prison, I am not free.

Eugene V. Debs

Comedy

There are only three basic jokes, but since the mother-in-law joke is not a joke but a very serious question, there are only two.

George Ade

Some people are so dry that you might soak them in a joke for a month and it would not get through their skins.

Henry Ward Beecher

People say to me, "Tell the truth. Was Will-Yum your own little boy?" And I confess that, no, he was my two girls, the kid next door, a good chunk of my childhood, and every kid I've ever seen in every kid-type misery and happiness. Will-Yum, I think, was every grown-up's trip backward to that peanut-butter-and-jelly world.

Dave Gerard

If you think before you speak, the other fellow gets in his joke first.

Edgar W. Howe

Don't tell a good story even though you know one; its narration will simply remind your hearers of a bad one.

Howe

The fellow that tells a good story always has to listen to a couple of poor ones.

Frank McKinney (Kin) Hubbard

I don't like the comedian image—the feeling that I'm the court jester who comes out after the banquet to make people laugh.

David Letterman

Back of every good belly laugh there is a familiarity with things not funny at all.

—Carole Lombard

The test of a real comedian is whether you laugh at him before he opens his mouth.

George Jean Nathan

I locked my keys in the car and had to break the windshield to get my wife out.

Red Skelton

Commerce

The commerce of the world is conducted by the strong, and usually it operates against the weak.

Henry Ward Beecher

How many pretenses men that sell good weave. What poor articles, with what a good face, do they palm off on their customers.

Beecher

In purchasing a drink of whisky at an ordinary bar, always lay down a half dollar. The barkeeper will then return to you a quarter and a dime, and there is a chance that the quarter will be a five-dollar piece. We cannot recommend this plan, however, as a means of growing rich; we have known several worthy gentlemen who have acted upon it with unswerving constancy for a long series of years and are no more affluent than when they began. It is absolutely essential to have some other income.

Ambrose Bierce

Piracy: Commerce without its folly-swaddles—just as God made it.

Bierce

Commerce: A kind of transaction in which A plunders from B the goods of C, and for compensation B picks the pocket of D of money belonging to E.

Bierce

Tariff: A scale of taxes on imports, designed to protect the domestic producer against the greed of his consumer.

Bierce

Merchant: One engaged in a commercial pursuit. A commercial pursuit is one in which the thing pursued is the dollar.

Bierce

Wealth and commerce are timid creatures; they must be assured that the nest will be safe before they build.

Benjamin Harrison

I pity that man who wants a coat so cheap that the man or woman who produces the cloth shall starve in the process.

Harrison

If you are content, I am not, that the nations of Europe shall absorb nearly the entire commerce of these near sister republics that lie to the south of us. It is naturally in large measure ours—ours by neighborhood, ours by nearness of access, ours by that sympathy that binds a hemisphere without a king.

Harrison

Nothing is as irritating as the fellow that chats pleasantly while he's overcharging you.

Frank McKinney (Kin) Hubbard

Don't a fellow feel good after he gets out of a store where he nearly bought something?

Hubbard

It seems like you can't buy anything any more that lasts as long as the old one.

Hubbard

The prudent, penniless beginner in the world labors for wages for awhile, saves a surplus with which to buy tools or land for himself another while, and at length hires another new beginner to help him. This is the just and generous and prosperous system that opens the way to all, gives hope to all, and consequently energy, progress, and improvement of conditions to all.

Abraham Lincoln

Many reasons may be assigned for the amazing economic development of the United States. . . . In my judgment the greatest factor has been, that there was created here in America the largest area in the world in which there were no barriers to the exchange of goods and ideas.

Wendell L. Willkie

Communism

You can't go slightly communist any more than you can become slightly leprous or slightly dead.

George N. Craig

There is not room enough in America for both the American Legion and communism, and the American Legion does not intend to move out.

Craig

This country today is in the hands of a secret inner coterie . . . which is directed by agents of the Soviet Union. . . . Our only choice is to impeach President [Harry] Truman to find out who is the secret invisible government.

William E. Jenner

The Divine Law is against communism.

Earl F. Landgrebe

We fight any enemy the President designates. We don't just keep talking communism, communism, communism. You might build up hate against one enemy and find yourself fighting another.

David M. Shoup

I want to tell you, I don't think the whole of Southeast Asia, as related to the present and future safety and freedom of the people of this country, is worth the life or limb of a single American.

Shoup

Our country is filled with socialistic, IWW, communistic, radicals, lawless, anti-American, anti-Church, anti-God, anti-marriage gangs and they are laying the eggs of rebellion and unrest in labor and capital and home; and we have some of them in the universities. I can take you back through the universities and pick out a lot of black-hearted communistic fellows who are teaching that to the boys and sending them out to undermine America. If this radical bunch could have their way, my friends, the laws of nature would be repealed, or they would reverse them. Oil and water would mix, the turtle dove would marry the turkey buzzard, the sun would rise in the west and set in the east, chickens would give milk and cows would lay eggs, the pigs would crow and the roosters would squeal, cats would bark and dogs would mew, the least would be the greatest, a part would be greater than the whole, yesterday would be today if that crowd were in control.

William Ashley (Billy) Sunday

Compliments

No one has ever been able to cash a compliment.

Edgar W. Howe

Compliment some men, and they will consider that there was nothing else to say.

Howe

You can't say anything complimentary to a woman that will surprise her.

Howe

Some folks pay a compliment like they went down in their pocket for it.

Frank McKinney (Kin) Hubbard

Some people pay a compliment as if they expect a receipt.

Hubbard

Conduct

Adherent: A follower who has not yet gotten all he expects.

Ambrose Bierce

Abnormal: Not conforming to standard. In matters of thought and conduct, to be independent is to be abnormal.

Bierce

I have never advocated violence in any form, I have always believed in education, in intelligence, in enlightenment, and I have always made my appeal to the reason and to the conscience of the people.

Eugene V. Debs

The louder a fellow laughs at nothing, the more popular he is.

Frank McKinney (Kin) Hubbard

I may be wrong in regard to any or all of them [opinions expressed] but, holding it a sound maxim that it is better only some times to be right than at all times to be wrong, so soon as I discover my opinions to be erroneous, I shall be ready to renounce them.

Abraham Lincoln

I shall try to correct errors when shown to be errors and I shall adopt new views as fast as they appear to be true views.

Lincoln

Conscience

The voice of conscience has a difficult time making connections with the ears.

Edgar W. Howe

Constitution

The movement for the Constitution of the United States was originated and carried through principally by four groups of personal interests . . . money, public securities, manufactures, and trade and shipping.

Charles A. Beard

The Constitution is essentially an economic document based upon the concept that the fundamental rights of private property are anterior to government and morally beyond the reach of popular majorities.

Beard

The members of the Philadelphia conventions that drafted the Constitution were, with a few exceptions, immediately, directly, and personally interested in, and derived economic advantages from the establishment of the new system.

Beard

As the patriots of Seventy-six did to the support of the Declaration of Independence, so to the support of the Constitution and the laws let every American pledge his life, his property, and his sacred honor; let every man remember that to violate the law is to trample on the blood of his father, and to tear the charter of his own and his children's liberty.

Abraham Lincoln

I hold that, in contemplation of universal law and the Constitution, the union of these states is perpetual. Perpetuity is implied, if not expressed, in the fundamental law of all national governments.

Lincoln

This country, with its institutions, belongs to the people who inhabit it. Whenever they shall grow weary of the existing government, they can exercise their constitutional right of amending it, or their revolutionary right to dismember or overthrow it.

Lincoln

Courage

Courage is the price that life exacts for granting peace.

Amelia Earhart

You needn't go to war to test your courage—have your teeth fixed.

Edgar W. Howe

Cowards

To sin by silence when they should protest makes cowards out of men.

Abraham Lincoln

Crime

Accomplice: One associated with another in a crime, having guilty knowledge and complicity, as an attorney who defends a criminal, knowing him guilty. This view of the attorney's position in the matter has not hitherto commanded the assent of attorneys, no one having offered them a fee for assenting.

Ambrose Bierce

Felon: A person of greater enterprise than discretion, who in embracing an opportunity has formed an unfortunate attachment.

Bierce

Trial: A formal inquiry designed to prove and put upon record the blameless characters of judges, advocates, and jurors.

Bierce

Abscond: To "move in a mysterious way," commonly with the property of another.

Bierce

Misdemeanor: An infraction of the law having less dignity than a felony and constituting no claim to admittance into the best criminal society.

Bierce

Gallows: A stage for the performance of miracle plays in which the leading actor is translated to heaven. In this country the gallows is chiefly remarkable for the number of persons who escape it.

Bierce

Prison: A place for punishments and rewards.

Bierce

Pardon: To remit a penalty and restore to a life of crime. To add to the lure of crime the temptation of ingratitude.

Bierce

I guess my only bad habit is robbing banks. I smoke very little and don't drink much.

John Dillinger

They're giving bank robbing a bad name.

Dillinger
on Bonnie and Clyde

Many a man is saved from being a thief by finding everything locked up. —Edgar W. Howe

Be careful, and you will save many men from the sin of robbing you.

Howe

I am a candidate for sheriff and if you elect me, and any of you need hanging while I am in office, I will hang you dead as hell.

Isaac Kirkendall
Kosciusko County
candidate, 1836

No man can hold my stolen horse long enough to get title to it.

Thomas R. Marshall

There is a quite current belief that if a man steals enough he can go scot-free; that it is only the moderate-minded thief who ever gets into trouble.

Marshall

You may fine me, but I intend to sell whisky till hell freezes over.

Katy Stoff
tried as tavern
keeper, 1867

Criticism

Critic: A person who boasts himself hard to please because nobody tried to please him.

Ambrose Bierce

Don't abuse your friends and expect them to consider it criticism.

Edgar W. Howe

He has a right to criticize, who has a heart to help.

Abraham Lincoln

Impersonal criticism . . . is like an impersonal fist fight or an impersonal marriage, and as successful.

George Jean Nathan

The dramatic critic who is without prejudice is on the plane with the general who does not believe in taking human life.

Nathan

Criticism is the art wherewith a critic tries to guess himself into a share of the artist's fame.

Nathan

Show me a critic without prejudices and I'll show you an arrested cretin.

Nathan

Criticism is the prevailing of intelligent skepticism over vague and befuddled prejudice and uncertainty.

Nathan

I'm a great devil's advocate. I can pierce holes through anything.

Marilyn Quayle

The critics have said everything they can, yet all they've made is a little sharp scratching, a little defacement.

Booth Tarkington

Because English majors can scarcely sign their own names at the end of a course of English instruction, many become serious critics.

Kurt Vonnegut

Curiosity

Half the world does not know how the other half lives but is trying to find out.

Edgar W. Howe

Cynicism

The cynic puts all human actions into two classes; openly bad and secretly bad.

Henry Ward Beecher

The cynic is the human owl, vigilant in darkness, and blind to light, mousing for vermin and never seeing noble game.

Beecher

Cynic: A blackguard whose faulty vision sees things as they are, not as they ought to be.

Ambrose Bierce

It'll soon be time for Christmas jewelry to turn green.

Frank McKinney (Kin) Hubbard

You never see no "to let" signs on Easy Street.

Hubbard

It is only the cynicism that is born of success that is penetrating and valid.

George Jean Nathan

Death

In the city a funeral is just an interruption in traffic; in the country it is a form of popular entertainment.

George Ade

What the mother sings at the cradle goes all the way down to the coffin.

Henry Ward Beecher

Death is not the end; there remains the litigation.

Ambrose Bierce

Grave: A place in which the dead are laid to await the coming of the medical student.

Bierce

Funeral: A pageant whereby we attest our respect for the dead by enriching the undertaker.

Bierce

Cemetery: An isolated suburban spot where mourners trade lies.

Bierce

Longevity: Uncommon extension of the fear of death.

Bierce

Mausoleum: The final and funniest folly of the rich.

Bierce

Epitaph: An inscription on a tomb showing that virtues acquired by death have a retroactive effect.

Bierce

Eulogy: Praise of a person who has either the advantage of wealth and power, or the consideration to be dead.

Bierce

Embalm: To cheat vegetation by locking up the gases upon which it feeds.

Bierce

Hearse: Death's baby carriage.

Bierce

I know I have lived before, many times, and I will live again. That's why death isn't a big deal any longer.

Joyce DeWitt

Hooray for the last great adventure! I wish I had won but it was worthwhile anyway.

Amelia Earhart
in a letter opened
after her death

If we die, we want people to accept it. We are in a risky business and we hope that if anything happens to us it will not delay the program. The conquest of space is worth the risk of life.

Virgil I. (Gus) Grissom

I can't die until the government finds a safe place to bury my liver.

Phil Harris

What a strange and tragic fate it has been of mine, to stand by the bier of three of my best friends, Lincoln, Garfield and McKinley, all done to death by assassins.

John Milton Hay

Funerals are a lost art in the big cities.

Don Herold

It seems to be human nature to attempt to get all the pleasure possible out of death.

Herold

When a man dies and his kin are glad of it, they say, "He's better off."

Edgar W. Howe

If a man dies and leaves his estate in an uncertain condition, the lawyers become his heirs.

Howe

What a scandal it would cause if an undertaker gave way to cheerfulness and whistled at his work.

Howe

Don't slander the dead: if you do justice to the living you will be kept busy.

Howe

By the time a man is ready to die, he is fit to live.

Howe

There should be something said on tombstones about husbands having been good providers, and less about love.

Howe

When a woman becomes a widow, she always tells you how young she was when she married.

Howe

The cemetery is a form of beauty I do not care for.

Howe

He took his first holiday in forty years yesterday, and picked out a cemetery plot.

Frank McKinney (Kin) Hubbard

To me death is not a fearful thing. It's living that's cursed.

James Warren (Jim) Jones

It is beautiful to die.

Jones

If they do kill me, I shall never die another death.

Abraham Lincoln

Death is a lengthened prayer, a longer night, a larger end. —Joaquin Miller

It proves what they always say; give the public what they want to see and they'll come out for it.

Red Skelton
on the crowd at
a producer's funeral

It's a very mixed blessing to be brought back from the dead.

Kurt Vonnegut

I myself will get an obituary in an Indianapolis paper when I die because I am related to people who used to own a chain of hardware stores.

Vonnegut

The monuments of the nations are all protests against nothingness after death; so are statues and inscriptions; so is history.

Lew Wallace

Dying is a short horse and soon curried. Living is a horse of another color and bigger.

Jessamyn West

Deathbed

Let me go. The world is bobbing around me. . . . The world is a bubble. Trouble wherever you go.

Sam Bass

Now comes the mystery.

Henry Ward Beecher

I cannot die: I have not finished my work.

James B. Eads

KHAQQ calling Itasca. We must be on you, but cannot see you. Gas is running low.

Amelia Earhart

Doctor . . . my lungs.

Benjamin Harrison

Sir, I wish you to understand the three principles of government. I wish them carried out. I ask nothing more.

William Henry Harrison
to Vice President John Tyler

The judge is doing all right.

Kenesaw Mountain Landis

I am dying. I am sworn out.

Oliver P. Morton

Relief has come.

Robert Owen

I am ready to meet my maker. [Sometimes reported as: Thy will be done.]

Lew Wallace

We meet in Heaven.

Wallace
to his wife

This is the end . . . I am dying . . . I can't bear up much longer. . . . Bury me here on the hill—by the flagpole.

Anthony Wayne

* * * *

These quotes, although not made on deathbeds, are among the late-in-life communications from these Hoosiers.

Tell my former friends in New York that the old man looks as if he might live ten years longer.

Charles Beard
a few days before his
death in 1948

As to me, I leave here tomorrow for an unknown destination.

Ambrose Bierce
in one of his last letters
home in 1913

You know, my fun days are over.

James Dean
a few days before his
death at age twenty-four

Shakespeare, here I come.

Theodore Dreiser
once suggested by him
as his epitaph

I don't need bodyguards.

Jimmy Hoffa
in an interview a month
before he disappeared

Definitions

The difference between perseverance and obstinacy is, that one often comes from a strong will, and the other from a strong won't.

Henry Ward Beecher

Gratitude is a dog licking the hand of the bread giver. There may be a few crumbs adhering to the fingers.

Ambrose Bierce

A specialist is one who knows everything about something and nothing about anything.

Bierce

Democracy

The real democratic idea is, not that every man shall be on a level with every other, but that every one shall have liberty, without hindrance, to be what God made him.

Henry Ward Beecher

We Americans have no commission from God to police the world.

Benjamin Harrison

A typical small town in the valley of Democracy, where people have their feet on the ground and their eyes on the stars.

Will H. Hays
commenting on
Sullivan, Indiana

Desires

Men have a thousand desires to a bushel of choices.

Henry Ward Beecher

The American people can have anything they want; the trouble is they don't know what they want. At least they vote that way on election day.

Eugene V. Debs

It always seemed to me that no one ever wanted me enough, unless it was my mother.

Theodore Dreiser

I want to do it because I want to do it.

Amelia Earhart

I was not accustomed to flattery. I was rather like the Hoosier with the gingerbread—who reckoned he loved it better than any man, and got less of it.

Abraham Lincoln

People prefer to be amused rather than reformed.

John T. McCutcheon

Every community has its dissenters, protestants, kickers, cranks; the more the merrier. My town has not lacked impressive examples, and I early formed a high resolve to strive for membership in their execrated company.

Meredith Nicholson

All I wanted to do was, number one, to get myself healthy. Number two, I would be able to help other people. And if I can succeed in any of those two, I'll feel like my mission has been accomplished.

William J. Schroeder

I'd rather have a lot of talent and a little experience than a lot of experience and little talent.

John Wooden

Diplomacy

Diplomacy: The patriotic art of lying for one's country.

Ambrose Bierce

Ultimatum: In diplomacy, a last demand before resorting to concessions.

Bierce

Compromise: Such an adjustment of conflict of interests as gives each adversary the satisfaction of thinking he has got what he ought not to have, and is deprived of nothing except what was justly his due.

Bierce

A diplomat is a fellow that lets you do all the talking while he gets what he wants.

Frank McKinney (Kin) Hubbard

Tact: The ability to describe others as they see themselves.

Abraham Lincoln

Discovery

The unthankful heart . . . discovers no mercies; but let the thankful heart sweep through the day and, as the magnet finds the iron, so it will find, in every hour, some heavenly blessings!

Henry Ward Beecher

Exploration is really the essence of the human spirit and I hope that we never forget it.

Frank Borman

The moon is a different thing to each one of us. It looks like a vast, lonely, forbidding place, an expanse of nothing.

Borman

Occasionally, I lie in bed at night and think now why in the hell do I want to get up on that thing?

Virgil I. (Gus) Grissom

If you go long enough without a bath, even the fleas will let you alone. —Ernie Pyle

Gentlemen, I regret Queen Hetepheres is not receiving.

George Andrew Reisner
on finding the queen's tomb empty
March 1927

When you awaken some morning and hear that somebody or other has been discovered, you can put it down as a fact that he discovered himself years ago—

since which time he has been working, toiling, and striving to make himself worthy of general discovery.

James Whitcomb Riley

Dislikes

I don't like these cold, precise, perfect people, who, in order not to speak wrong, never speak at all, and in order not to do wrong, never do anything.

Henry Ward Beecher

I do not believe in doing for pleasure things that I do not like to do.

Don Herold

Lord, spare me from sickly women and healthy men.

Herold

If anyone dislikes you, you can overcome his dislike by asking him for any kind of information.

Edgar W. Howe

The worse sensation I know of is getting up in the night and stepping on a toy train of cars.

Frank McKinney (Kin) Hubbard

I don't think much of a dance step where the girl looks like she was being carried out of a burning building.

Hubbard

I don't approve of open fires: you can't think, or talk, or even make love in front of a fireplace—all you can do is stare at it.

Rex Stout

Doctrine

Doctrine is nothing but the skin of truth set up and stuffed.

Henry Ward Beecher

Radicalism: The conservatism of tomorrow injected into the affairs of today.

Ambrose Bierce

I would a thousand times rather march under the bloody shirt, stained with the lifeblood of a Union soldier, than to march under the black flag of treason or the white flag of compromise.

Benjamin Harrison

The scientists are the world's greatest army devoted to good works. . . . In a world filled with men who shamefully invent fables to uphold their opinions or defend their guilt, the scientists attack falseness of every kind, and accept no doctrine until the last doubt has been disposed of.

Edgar W. Howe

As I would not be a slave, so I would not be a master. This expresses my idea of democracy.

Abraham Lincoln

Dogma

Think of the dull functioning of dogma, age after age. How many millions have been led shunting along dogmatic runways from the dark into the dark again . . . endless billions, and at the gates, dogma, ignorance, vice, cruelty, seize them and clamp this or that band upon their brains.

Theodore Dreiser

Nothing is as dogmatic as sincere ignorance.

Max Ehrmann

That one man or ten thousand or ten million men find a dogma acceptable does not argue for its soundness.

David Starr Jordan

The dogmas of the quiet past are inadequate to the stormy present. As our case is new, so we must think and act anew. We must disenthrall ourselves, and then we shall save our country.

Abraham Lincoln

Drama

I wanted to be an actress because that was the thing I was best at. I knew I could do it. There are very few things in life that we know we can do.

Anne Baxter

Dramatist: One who adapts plays from the French.

Ambrose Bierce

Pantomime: A play in which the story is told without violence to the language.

Bierce

Great drama is the reflection of a great doubt in the heart and mind of a great, sad, gay man.

George Jean Nathan

Charlton Heston, a pretty fellow whom the moving pictures should exultantly capture without delay if they have any respect for the dramatic stage, duly adjusts his chemise so the audience may swoon over his expansive, hirsute chest and conducts his prize physique about the platform like a physical culture demonstrator.

Nathan

Drama—what literature does at night.

Nathan

All really great drama is a form of scandal.

Nathan

It isn't a shortage of good scripts that ails the theater; it is a shortage of producers who know a good script when they see one.

Nathan

Fantasy is weak, serious drama filtered through a poetic imagination into beauty.

Nathan

The theater is an undying institution because it educates its audience's emotions.

Nathan

A triumph of sugar over diabetes.

Nathan
of playwright J. M. Barrie

Drink

Wine, madam, is God's next best gift to man.

Ambrose Bierce

Whoever takes just plain ginger ale soon gets drowned out of the conversation.

Frank McKinney (Kin) Hubbard

Alcoholic psychosis is nothing more or less than ole D.T.'s in a dinner suit.

Hubbard

Dr. Knapp of Berlin, Germany, has discovered a cure for red noses, but then a fellow that boozes wouldn't waste money on an ocean trip.

Hubbard

Beverage alcohol has many defenders but no defense.

Abraham Lincoln

I drink to make other people interesting.

George Jean Nathan

Drink the first. Sip the second slowly. Skip the third.

Knute Rockne

Good-bye John [Barleycorn]. You were God's worst enemy. You were hell's best friend.

William Ashley (Billy) Sunday

I'm going to fight the liquor business till hell freezes over, and then I'll put on ice skates and fight it some more.

Sunday

There are two things that will be believed of any man whatsoever, and one of them is that he has taken to drink.

Booth Tarkington

Duty

He who is false to present duty breaks a thread in the loom, and will find the flaw when he may have forgotten its cause.

Henry Ward Beecher

Duty: That which sternly impels us in the direction of profit, along the line of desire.

Ambrose Bierce

There is a great sense of loneliness in the discharge of high public duties. The moment of decision is one of isolation.

Benjamin Harrison

I declare my belief that it is not your duty to do anything that is not to your own interest. Whenever it is unquestionably your duty to do a thing, then it will benefit you to perform that duty.

Edgar W. Howe

Let us have faith that right makes might, and in that faith let us to the end dare to do our duty as we understand it.

Abraham Lincoln

No one does his duty unless he does his best.

William Ashley (Billy) Sunday

Earth

Today the pressure is on, but we have a choice. Mankind can either lie down and give up, or we can use all of our productive skills and knowledge to work for a better future.

Earl L. Butz

If the meek ever do inherit the earth some one will get it away from them before they have it an hour.

Frank McKinney (Kin) Hubbard

Economy

You know what an economist is—he is a man with a watch chain with a Phi Beta Kappa key on it but no watch to put in his vest pocket.

Roger Branigin

Our capitalism is no longer capitalism; it is a weakened mixture of government regulations and limited business opportunities.

Earl L. Butz

Economic independence doesn't set anyone free. Or it shouldn't. For the higher you go, the more responsibilities become yours.

Bernard F. Gimbel

Buying material, clothing, bacon, radishes, onions—a few more warm days and everything will be up.

Frank McKinney (Kin) Hubbard

All morons who are in office loudly claim to be economists.

John N. Hurty

Capital has its rights, which are as worthy of protection as any other rights.

Abraham Lincoln

Labor is prior to, and independent of, capital. Capital is only the fruits of labor. . . . Labor is the superior of capital, and deserves much higher consideration.

Lincoln

Education

"Whom are you?" he asked, for he had been to night school.

George Ade

What education does is to make a tool of every faculty—how to open it, how to keep it sharp, and how to apply it to all practical purposes.

Henry Ward Beecher

Education: That which discloses to the wise and disguises from the foolish their lack of understanding.

Ambrose Bierce

Academy: A modern school where football is taught.

Bierce

Erudition: Dust shaken out of a book into an empty skull. —Bierce

After centuries of education we still have plenty of primitives—some of them white-collar or even top-hat primitives . . . people who seem actuated only by hatred and fear and envy.

Elmer H. Davis

You could close every university in the United States and it wouldn't make any difference. You can get a degree today on the most asinine subjects you ever heard of—most of the youngsters are sneaking and cheating their way through school. None of the schools is worth a damn except the technical schools.

Theodore Dreiser

Education was early in the thoughts of the framers of our Constitution as one of the best, if not the only guarantee of their perpetuation. . . . How shall one be a safe citizen when citizens are rulers who are not intelligent? How shall he understand those great questions which his suffrage must adjudge without thorough intellectual culture in his youth?

Benjamin Harrison

I had, out of my sixty teachers, a scant half dozen who couldn't have been supplanted by phonographs.

Don Herold

Pasadena [California] lecture course halls are heated by high blood pressure.

Herold

It is hard to convince a high school student that he will encounter a lot of problems more difficult than those of algebra and geometry.

Edgar W. Howe

If there were no schools to take the children away from home part of the time, the insane asylum would be filled with mothers.

Howe

Half of the little education people have is usually wrong.

Howe

I never graduated from Iowa, but I was only there two terms—Truman's and Eisenhower's.

Alex Karras

You don't walk in and out of geology class and cheer when a guy does the right problem on the board.

Robert Montgomery (Bobby) Knight
on the attitude of sports fans

Upon the subject of education, not presuming to dictate any plan or system respecting it, I can only say that I view it as the most important subject that we, as a people, can be engaged in.

Abraham Lincoln

In the speech of the illiterate, there is usually something of rhythm and cadence.

Meredith Nicholson

We're going to have the best educated American people in the world.

Danford Quayle

That's fine phonetically, but you're missing just a little bit.

Quayle
on adding an e to spell potato

My school life was a farce all the way through.

James Whitcomb Riley

The rivers of America will run with blood filled to their banks before we will submit to them taking the Bible out of our schools.

William Ashley (Billy) Sunday

Just because some of us can read and write and do a little math, that doesn't mean we deserve to conquer the universe.

Kurt Vonnegut

Educating a beautiful woman is like pouring honey into a fine Swiss watch: everything stops.

Vonnegut

Education is the mother of leadership.

Wendell L. Willkie

Ego

Do not give, as many men do, like a hen that lays her eggs and then cackles.

Henry Ward Beecher

Conceit is the most incurable disease that is known to the human soul.

Beecher

Egotist: A person of low taste, more interested in himself than in me.

Ambrose Bierce

Self-esteem: An erroneous appraisement.

Bierce

They say that hens do cackle loudest when there's nothing vital in the eggs they've laid.

Bierce

Flatter: To impress another with a sense of one's own merit.

Bierce

The cemeteries of the world are full of indispensable men and women, but somehow the world goes on.

Theodore Hesburgh

An ego is just imagination. And if a man doesn't have imagination he'll be working for somebody else for the rest of his life.

Jimmy Hoffa

When I say "everybody says so," I mean I say so.

Edgar W. Howe

There are too many folks of limited means who think that nothing is too good for them.

Frank McKinney (Kin) Hubbard

Egotism is the anesthetic that dulls the pain of stupidity.

Frank Leahy

It is difficult to make a man miserable while he feels he is worthy of himself and claims kindred to the great God who made him.

Abraham Lincoln

Elections

No matter who wins, the people are always worsted in an election.

Edgar W. Howe

Emotions

A man never feels more important than when he receives a telegram containing more than ten words.

George Ade

Anxiety in human life is what squeaking and grinding are in machinery that is not oiled. In life, trust is the oil.

Henry Ward Beecher

In things pertaining to enthusiasm, no man is sane who does not know how to be insane on the proper occasion.

Beecher

Tears are often the telescopes by which men see far into heaven.

Beecher

All fishes, of course, lack the mimetic or facial muscles so characteristic of the mammals, and are therefore unable to express their emotions above the neck. The emotions of most fishes would be difficult to express, anyway.

William Jacob Cuppy

Every beginner feels or really finds that the doors are more or less closed against him.

Theodore Dreiser

Perhaps no emotion cools sooner than that of gratitude.

Benjamin Harrison

It takes a lot of time to be sentimental.

Don Herold

Pleasure is more trouble than trouble.

Herold

Spirit is the root of personality.

Theodore Hesburgh

Nobody ever grew despondent looking for trouble.

Frank McKinney (Kin) Hubbard

Kindness goes a long ways lots of times when it ought to stay at home.

Hubbard

No one can feel as helpless as the owner of a sick goldfish.

Hubbard

[I feel] somewhat like the boy in Kentucky who stubbed his toe while running to see his sweetheart. The boy said he was too big to cry, and far too badly hurt to laugh.

Abraham Lincoln
on a political loss

My heart is a stone: heavy with sadness for my people; cold with the knowledge that no treaty will keep the whites out of our lands; hard with the determination to resist as long as I live and breathe. Now we are weak and many of our people are afraid. But hear me: a single twig breaks, but the bundle of twigs is strong. Some day I will embrace our brother tribes and draw them into a bundle and together we will win our country back from the whites.

Tecumseh
speech at Vincennes, 1810

Laughing or crying is what a human being does when there's nothing else he can do.

Kurt Vonnegut

A good time for laughing is when you can.

Jessamyn West

The source of one's joy is also often the source of one's sorrow.

West

Enemies

When you are ill make haste to forgive your enemies, for you may recover.

Ambrose Bierce

Enemy: A designing scoundrel who has done you some service that is inconvenient to repay. In military affairs a body of men actuated by the basest motives and pursuing the most iniquitous aims.

Bierce

Outdo: To make an enemy.

Bierce

Contempt: The feeling of a prudent man for an enemy who is too formidable safely to be opposed.

Bierce

Pitiful: The state of an enemy or opponent after an imaginary encounter with oneself.

Bierce

It's always been my theory that you keep the door open to your enemies. You know all about your friends.

Jimmy Hoffa

If you knew how cowardly your enemy is, you would slap him. Bravery is knowledge of the cowardice in the enemy.

Edgar W. Howe

If you attend to your work and let your enemy alone, someone else will come along some day and do him up for you.

Howe

Instead of loving your enemies, treat your friends a little better.

Howe

You needn't love your enemy, but if you refrain from telling lies about him, you are doing well enough.

Howe

Am I not destroying my enemies when I make friends of them?

Abraham Lincoln

Entertainment

Entertainment: Any kind of amusement whose inroads stop short of death by dejection.

Ambrose Bierce

A man never does justice to himself as an entertainer when his wife is around.

Edgar W. Howe

The only way to amuse some people is to slip and fall on an icy pavement.

Howe

The only way to entertain some folks is to listen to them.

Frank McKinney (Kin) Hubbard

Saturday night, there wasn't anything for us to do in my hometown but go down to the barbershop and watch a few haircuts.

Herb Shriner

Ethics

Hold yourself responsible for a higher standard than anybody else expects of you. Never excuse yourself. Never pity yourself. Be a hard master to yourself—and be lenient to everybody else.

Henry Ward Beecher

Responsibility: A detachable burden easily shifted to the shoulders of God, fate, fortune, luck, or one's neighbors.

Ambrose Bierce

Evil

Of two evils, choose to be the least.

Ambrose Bierce

The evils of tyranny are rarely seen but by him who resists it. —John Milton Hay

In giving the devil his due, you are liable to give yourself away.

Edgar W. Howe

Say what you will about the devil, he's a hustler.

Frank McKinney (Kin) Hubbard

If there were only some shorter and more direct route to the devil, it would save an awful lot of sorrow and anxiety in this world.

Hubbard

I have often wondered how much of the general fund of evil in this world comes from thoughtlessness. Cultivate thought and you make a virtue.

Charles Major

The way, and the only way, to check and stop this evil, is for all the red men to unite in claiming a common and equal right in the land, as it was at first and should be yet; for it was never divided, but belongs to all for the use of each. . . . That no part has a right to sell, even to each other, much less to strangers—those who want all and will not do with less.

Tecumseh
speech at Vincennes, 1810

I merely wish to reiterate that atomic bombs are evil and that they cannot be used to maintain peace.

Harold C. Urey

Excuses

Tell them I don't have any clean underwear.

Roger Branigin
rejecting an invitation
to the White House

He reminds me of the man who murdered both his parents, and then, when sentence was about to be pronounced, pleaded for mercy on the grounds that he was an orphan.

Abraham Lincoln

Experience

Customs represent the experiences of mankind.

Henry Ward Beecher

Experience is a revelation in the light of which we renounce our errors of youth for those of age.

Ambrose Bierce

Experience: The wisdom that enables us to recognize in an undesirable old acquaintance the folly that we have already embraced.

Bierce

Some people have nothing else but experience.

Don Herold

Nothing is wonderful when you get used to it.

Edgar W. Howe

Another distinguishing feature about the school of experience is this—when you're through you're through.

Frank McKinney (Kin) Hubbard

I do not mean to say we are bound to follow implicitly in whatever our fathers did. To do so, would be to discard all the lights of current experience—to reject all progress, all improvement.

Abraham Lincoln

Expertise

One of the things that is wrong with America is that everybody who has done anything at all in his own field is expected to be an authority on every other subject under the sun.

Elmer H. Davis

Failure

Failure is a school in which the truth always grows strong.

Henry Ward Beecher

To the eye of failure, success is an accident with a presumption of crime.

Ambrose Bierce

Failure must be but a challenge to others.

Amelia Earhart

The woman who has been married and divorced a number of times reminds us of the man who is always failing in business.

Edgar W. Howe

The fellow that tries to commit suicide with a razor, and fails, would fail at anything.

Frank McKinney (Kin) Hubbard

A failure must have a hard time tracing his downfall in a dry town.

Hubbard

Why they call a fellow who keeps losing all the time a good sport gets me.

Hubbard

The probability that we may fail in the struggle ought not to deter us from the support of a cause we believe to be just.

Abraham Lincoln

What is there to be afraid of? The worse thing that can happen is you fail. So what? I failed at a lot of things. My first record was horrible.

John Cougar Mellencamp

More men fail through lack of purpose than through lack of talent.

William Ashley (Billy) Sunday

Faith

Faith is nothing but spiritualized imagination.

Henry Ward Beecher

Faith: Belief without evidence in what is told by one who speaks without knowledge, of things without parallel.

Ambrose Bierce

Faith is not an easy virtue; but, in the broad world of man's total voyage through time to eternity, faith is not only a gracious companion, but an essential guide.

Theodore Hesburgh

There are very few women who have as much faith in the Lord as a bride has in her husband.

Edgar W. Howe

Faith is something entirely possessed by children, and they don't know they have it.

Howe

Say what you will about the sweet miracle of unquestioning faith. I consider a capacity for it terrifying and absolutely vile.

Kurt Vonnegut

Fame

Famous: Conspicuously miserable.

Ambrose Bierce

Renown: A degree of distinction between notoriety and fame—a little more supportable than the one and a little more intolerable than the other.

Bierce

Fame and serenity can never be bedfellows.

James (Doc) Counsilman

But remember that fame in many cases is but the last few throbs of a broken heart.

Paul Dresser

Folks that become prominent and don't take a good photograph are certainly up against it.

Frank McKinney (Kin) Hubbard

Some folks are born great, others achieve greatness, and still others wear a wide braid on their nose glasses.

Hubbard

We were going to put up a statue for a local fellow who had gone off and got famous and then he never came back so we couldn't find out who he was.

Herb Shriner

Family

Every family has prize kin.

Edgar W. Howe

The family is the building block for whatever solidarity there is in society.

Jill Ruckelshaus

Fashion

My grandfather, Frank Lloyd Wright, wore a red sash on his wedding night. That is glamour!

Anne Baxter

Fashion: A despot whom the wise ridicule and obey.

Ambrose Bierce

Armor is the kind of clothing worn by a man whose tailor was a blacksmith.

Bierce

Garter: An elastic band intended to keep a woman from coming out of her stockings and desolating the country.

Bierce

Sometimes the eye gets so accustomed that if you don't have a change, you're bored. It's the same with fashion, you know. And that, I suppose, is what style is about.

Bill Blass

When in doubt, wear red.

Blass

Honey, if there's a part of the human body to exploit you might as well get onto it.

Blass

Design is like the theater—the bug bites you early.

Blass

They seem cool and comfortable and there is something about the air of a girl who wears them that reminds me of the Declaration of Independence.

Eugene V. Debs
on bloomers

No woman should have enough clothes to make her ask, "What'll I wear?"

Don Herold

When a man buys a new hat, he wants one just like the one he has had before. But a woman isn't that way.

Edgar W. Howe

One good thing about having one suit of clothes—you've always got your pencil.

Frank McKinney (Kin) Hubbard

The short skirts of today reveal the malnutrition of yesterday.

Hubbard

Fate

A door that seems to stand open must be of a man's size, or it is not the door that providence means for him.

Henry Ward Beecher

Destiny: A tyrant's authority for crime and a fool's excuse for failure.

Ambrose Bierce

Some folks get what's coming to them by waiting, others while crossing the street.

Frank McKinney (Kin) Hubbard

Lots of folks confuse bad management with destiny. —Hubbard

If rape is inevitable relax and enjoy it. I'm not talking about the act of rape, don't misinterpret me there. But what I'm talking about is something's happened to you so you have to handle it. You have to be able to realize there's nothing you can do about it.

Robert Montgomery (Bobby) Knight

A child is a person who is going to carry on what you have started. He is going to sit where you are sitting, and when you're gone, attend to those things that you think are important. . . . The fate of humanity is in his hands.

Abraham Lincoln

If destruction be our lot we must ourselves be its author and finisher. As a nation of free men we must live through all time, or die by suicide.

Lincoln

From the very first, I knew I had no chance to become a great man, because I wasn't born in a log cabin.

Ernie Pyle

Fear

The fear of doing right is the grand treason in times of danger.

Henry Ward Beecher

Fear secretes acids; but love and trust are sweet juices.

Beecher

Fear is the soul's signal for rallying.

Beecher

Coward: One who in a perilous emergency thinks with his legs.

Ambrose Bierce

Ghost: The outward and visible sign of an inward fear.

Bierce

If a man harbors any sort of fear, it percolates through all his thinking, damages his personality, makes him landlord to a ghost.

Lloyd C. Douglas

Many fears are born of fatigue and loneliness.

Max Ehrmann

People tolerate those they fear further than those they love.

Edgar W. Howe

I'm not afraid of death, nor of the damned old devil, but I am afraid of the time when I shall be compelled to sit on the front porch in the "lean and slippered pantaloon" and impotently watch the worlds go by.

John N. Hurty

We live in the midst of alarms; anxiety beclouds the future; we expect some new disaster with each newspaper we read.

Abraham Lincoln

Every morning when I wake up the first thought that comes to me is: This is the day they get on to me.

James Whitcomb Riley

Figures

Once: Enough.

Ambrose Bierce

Twice: Once too often.

Bierce

There are two kinds of statistics, the kind you look up and the kind you make up.

Rex Stout

Finance

Interest works night and day in fair weather and in foul. It gnaws at a man's substance with invisible teeth.

Henry Ward Beecher

In freeing peoples . . . our country's blessing will also come; for profit follows righteousness.

Albert J. Beveridge

Forgetfulness: A gift of God bestowed upon debtors in compensation for their destitution of conscience.

Ambrose Bierce

Creditor: One of a tribe of savages dwelling beyond the financial straits and dreaded for their desolating incursions.

Bierce

Ernest attention should be given to those combinations of capital commodity commonly called trusts.

Benjamin Harrison

Financial sense is knowing that certain men will promise to do certain things, and fail.

Edgar W. Howe

We don't want racetrack money, and our country and our exchanges will be better off if those who "play" the stock market on the basis of tips stay out.

Emil Schram

Folly

A good folly is worth whatever you pay for it.

George Ade

Folly: That gift . . . whose creative and controlling energy inspires man's mind, guides his actions and adorns his life.

Ambrose Bierce

Experience: The wisdom that enables us to recognize as an undesirable old acquaintance the folly that we have already embraced.

Bierce

I think some folks are foolish to pay what it costs to live.

Frank McKinney (Kin) Hubbard

It is an utterly foolish thing for one man to say what he would have done if he had been in another man's place, at another time. . . . I have always thought that if I had been Adam in the Garden of Eden I would not have eaten the apple—but I do not know. I never saw Eve, and for aught I know, had I been there, instead of merely taking a bite I might have endeavored to consume the entire crop.

Thomas R. Marshall

Food

Why is not a rat as good as a rabbit? Why should men eat shrimps and neglect cockroaches?

Henry Ward Beecher

Mayonnaise: One of the sauces which serve the French in place of a state religion.

Ambrose Bierce

Oyster: A slimy, goby shellfish that civilization gives men the hardihood to eat without removing its entrails. The shells are sometimes given to the poor.

Bierce

Edible: Good to eat, and wholesome to digest, as a worm to a toad, a toad to a snake, a snake to a pig, a pig to a man, and a man to a worm.

Bierce

Appetite: An instinct thoughtfully implanted by Providence as a solution to the labor question.

Bierce

Cannibal: A gastronome of the old school who preserves the simple tastes and adheres to the natural diet of the prepork period.

Bierce

Digestion: The conversion of victuals into virtues.

Bierce

Glutton: A person who escapes the evils of moderation by committing dyspepsia.

Bierce

Sauce: The one infallible sign of civilization and enlightenment. A people without sauces has one thousand vices; a people with one sauce has only nine hundred and ninety-nine.

Bierce

Food is a weapon . . . one of the principal tools in our negotiating kit.

Earl L. Butz

My one culinary talent lies in thinking up new and palatable ways of opening tin cans.

William Jacob Cuppy

We are indeed much more than we eat, but what we eat can nevertheless help us to be much more than what we are.

Adelle Davis

Eat breakfast like a king, lunch like a prince, and dinner like a pauper.

Davis

You can't eat well and keep fit if you don't shop well.

Davis

The longer I work in nutrition, the more convinced I become that for the healthy person all foods should be delicious.

Davis

To say that obesity is caused merely by consuming too many calories is like saying that the only cause of the American Revolution was the Boston Tea Party.

Davis

You should first give them a good dinner, then a good cussing whenever you want money.

Carl Graham Fisher

There is something in the red of a raspberry pie that looks as good to a man as the red in a sheep looks to a wolf.

Edgar W. Howe

The flavor of frying bacon beats orange blossoms.

Howe

Most people eat as though they were fattening themselves for the market.

Howe

We are always reminded of our favorite reform after dinner; it's that people eat too much.

Howe

When a man diets he eats oatmeal in addition to everything else he usually eats.

Howe

Put cream and sugar on a fly, and it tastes very much like a black raspberry.

Howe

A hot lemonade at night is good for almost every ill, from cold, headaches and grippe, to rheumatism. The people should quit trotting after doctors and devote more time to lemons.

Howe

Where the guests at a gathering are well acquainted, they eat 20 percent more than they otherwise would.

Howe

The better a pie tastes, the worse it is for you.

Howe

Lots of people insist on eating with a knife who were born with a silver spoon in their mouth.

Frank McKinney (Kin) Hubbard

There's somebody at every dinner party who eats all the celery.

Hubbard

There ought to be some way to eat celery so it wouldn't sound like you were stepping on a basket.

Hubbard

A bunch of nice celery makes a great decoy for a bum dining hall.

Hubbard

The easier something's prepared, the less a husband likes it.

Hubbard

The husband that uncomplainingly eats what's set before him may live more peacefully, but not as long.

Hubbard

It must be nice to run a boardinghouse and not have to worry about something different for dinner every day.

Hubbard

Men dig graves with their teeth.

John N. Hurty

The right of liberty and pursuing happiness secured by the Constitution embraces the right, in each compos mentis individual, of selecting what he will eat and drink.

Samuel E. Perkins
on Prohibition

The human animal who has access to nature's store of foods does not require a trained dietitian to write a menu for him. Inasmuch, however, as a large percentage of us have access only to prepared foods, it is well to be on our guard.

Harvey W. Wiley

Fools

Men are called fools in one age for not knowing what they were called fools for doing in the age before.

Henry Ward Beecher

I have known many an instance of a man writing a letter and forgetting to sign his name, but this is the only instance I have ever known of a man signing his name and forgetting to write the letter.

Beecher
upon getting a letter
that merely said "Fool"

The first man you meet is a fool; if you do not think so ask him, and he will prove it.

Ambrose Bierce

Fool: A person who pervades the domain of intellectual speculation and diffuses himself through the channels of moral activity. He is omnific, omniform, omniscient, omniscience, omnipotent.

Bierce

April fool: The March fool with another month added to his folly.

Bierce

Rascal: A fool considered under another aspect.

Bierce

Circus: a place where horses, ponies, and elephants are permitted to see men, women, and children acting the fool.

Bierce

Craft: A fool's substitute for brains.

Bierce

If the fools do not control the world, it isn't because they are not in the majority.

Edgar W. Howe

Don't be mean to a fool; put a penny in his cup, as you do for the blind beggar.

Howe

Whoever catches the fool first is entitled to shear him. —Howe

The majority of people display their individuality most in the kind of fool they become.

Howe

A fool will not only pay for a cure that does him no good, but he will write a testimonial that he was cured.

Howe

The only difference between this generation and my generation is that they have different ways of making fools of themselves.

Thomas R. Marshall

Only a fool would refuse to enter a fool's paradise—when that's the only paradise he'll ever have a chance to enter.

Jessamyn West

Forgiveness

"I can forgive, but I cannot forget," is only another way of saying, "I cannot forgive." Forgiveness ought to be like a cancelled note, torn in two and burned up, so that it can never be shown against the man.

Henry Ward Beecher

It is very easy to forgive others their mistakes. It takes more gut and gumption to forgive them for having witnessed your own.

Jessamyn West

Freedom

One of the best ways to get yourself a reputation as a dangerous citizen these days is to go about repeating the very phrases that our founding fathers used in the great struggle for independence.

Charles A. Beard

Liberty is the soul's right to breathe, and, when it cannot take a long breath, laws are girdled too tight.

Henry Ward Beecher

Perfect emancipation is effected only when the mind is permitted to form, to express, and to employ its own convictions of truth on all subjects, as it chooses.

Beecher

True obedience is true liberty.

Beecher

The things required for prosperous labor, prosperous manufacturers, and prosperous commerce are three: first, liberty; second, liberty; third, liberty.

Beecher

Freedom: Exemption from the stress of authority in a beggarly half dozen of restraint's infinite multitude of methods. The distinction between freedom and liberty is not accurately known; naturalists have never been able to find a living specimen of either.

Ambrose Bierce

Freedom is a political condition that every nation supposes itself to enjoy in virtual monopoly.

Bierce

Liberty: One of imagination's most precious possessions.

Bierce

What makes western civilization worth saving is the freedom of the mind, now under heavy attack from the primitives who have persisted among us. If we have not the courage to defend that faith, it won't matter much whether we are saved or not.

Elmer H. Davis

I realize that . . . there are certain limitations placed upon the right of free speech. I must be exceeding careful, prudent, as to what I say, and even more careful and prudent as to how I say it. I may not be able to say all I think, but I am not going to say anything I do not think.

Eugene V. Debs

Liberty, divinest word ever coined by human brain or uttered by human tongue. It is the spirit of liberty that today undermines the empires of the world, sets crowns and miters askew, and in its onward elemental sweep is shaking the institutions of capitalism in this nation as frail weeds are shaken in the blast of the storm king's fury.

Debs

Nothing is proved, all is permitted. Men will do what they think they can get away with.

Theodore Dreiser

The liberties of a people depend on their own constant attention to its preservation.

William Henry Harrison

I express many absurd opinions. But I am not the first man to do it; American freedom consists largely in talking nonsense.

Edgar W. Howe

I have never been free; the world, my kin, my neighbors have always enslaved me.

Howe

You often hear that this is a free country, and that a man is at liberty to express his opinions. It is not true.

Howe

We are not free; it was not intended we should be. A book of rules is placed in our cradle, and we never get rid of it until we reach our graves. Then we are free, and only then.

Howe

Those who deny freedom to others deserve it not for themselves.

Abraham Lincoln

I appeal to you to constantly bear in mind that not with politicians, not with presidents, not with office seekers, but with you is the question: Shall the Union and shall the liberties of this country be preserved to the latest generations?

Lincoln

My faith in the proposition that each man should do precisely as he pleases with all that is exclusively his own lies at the foundation of the sense of justice there is in me. I extend the principle to communities of men as well as to individuals.

Lincoln

The fight must go on. The cause of civil liberty must not be surrendered at the end of one or even one hundred defeats.

Lincoln

What constitutes the bulwark of our own liberty and independence? It is not our frowning battlements, our bristling sea coasts, the guns of our war steamers, or the strength of our gallant and disciplined army. Our reliance is in the love of liberty that God has implanted in us.

Lincoln

We will make converts day by day; we will grow strong by the violence and injustice of our adversaries. And, unless truth be a mockery and justice a hollow lie, we will be in the majority after awhile, and then the revolution that we will accomplish will be none the less radical from being the result of pacific measures. The battle of freedom is to be fought out on principal.

Lincoln

We all declare for liberty; but in using the same word, we do not all mean the same thing. With some, the word "liberty" may mean for each man to do as he pleases with himself and the product of his labor; while with others, the same word may mean for some men to do as they please with other men and the product of other men's labor. Here are two, not only different, but incomparable things, called by the same name—liberty. And it follows that each of the things is, by the respective parties, called by two different and incompatible names—liberty and tyranny.

Lincoln

We behold the process by which thousands are daily passing from under the yoke of bondage hailed by some as the advance of liberty, and bewailed by others as the destruction of liberty.

Lincoln

I intend no modification of my oft-expressed personal wish that all men everywhere could be free.

Lincoln

A great deal of the so-called government encroachment on the area of business, labor, and the professions has been asked for by the people misusing their freedom.

J. Irwin Miller

Freedom is an indivisible word. If we want to enjoy it, and fight for it, we must be prepared to extend it to everyone, whether they are rich or poor, whether they agree with us or not, no matter what their race or the color of their skin.

Wendell L. Willkie

Whenever we take away the liberties of those whom we hate we are opening the way to loss of liberty for those we love.

Willkie

When we talk of freedom and opportunity for all nations, the mocking paradoxes in our own society become so clear they can no longer be ignored. If we want to talk about freedom, we must mean freedom for others as well as ourselves, and we must mean freedom for everyone inside our frontiers as well as outside.

Willkie

The world is awake, at last, to the knowledge that the rule of people by other people is not freedom.

Willkie

Only the productive are strong, only the strong are free.

Willkie

Friendship

Every man should have a fair-sized cemetery in which to bury the faults of his friends.

Henry Ward Beecher

Acquaintance: A person whom we know well enough to borrow from, but not well enough to lend to. A degree of friendship called slight when its object is poor or obscure, and intimate when he is rich or famous.

Ambrose Bierce

Friendship: A ship big enough to carry two in fair weather, but only one in foul.

Bierce

Friendless: Having no favors to bestow. Destitute of fortune. Addicted to utterance of truth and common sense.

Bierce

Befriend: To make an ingrate.

Bierce

Benefactor: One who makes heavy purchases of ingratitude, without, however, materially affecting the price, which is still within the means of all.

Bierce

Think twice before you speak to a friend in need.

Bierce

Beggar: One who has relied on the assistance of his friends.

Bierce

While your friend holds you affectionately by both your hands you are safe, because you can watch both of his.

Bierce

Friends are the sunshine of life. —John Milton Hay

Make all good men your well-wishers, and then, in the years' steady sifting, some of them will turn into friends.

Hay

A friend that isn't in need is a friend indeed.

Frank McKinney (Kin) Hubbard

A fellow doesn't have over two or three real friends in a lifetime. Once in awhile you meet someone that's nice and clever; but he generally turns out to be an agent for something.

Hubbard

Probably no man ever had a friend he did not dislike a little; we are all so constituted by nature so no one can possibly entirely approve of us.

Edgar W. Howe

If a friend is in trouble, don't annoy him by asking if there is anything you can do. Think up something appropriate and do it.

Howe

A man's best friend is seldom his neighbor.

Howe

Friends are like a pleasant park where you wish to go; while you may enjoy the flowers, you may not eat them.

Howe

A friend is someone who has the same enemies you have.

Abraham Lincoln

To correct the evils, great and small, which spring from want of sympathy and from positive enmity among strangers, as nations or as individuals, is one of the highest functions of civilization.

Lincoln

If you would win a man to your cause, first convince him that you are his true friend. Therein is a drop of honey that catches his heart, which, say what he will, is the greatest high road to his reason, and which when once gained, you will find but little trouble in convincing his judgment of the justice of your cause if, indeed, that cause be really a just one.

Lincoln

Men use care in purchasing a horse and are neglectful in choosing friends.

John Muir

Fun

Debauchee: One who has so earnestly pursued pleasure that he has had the misfortune to overtake it.

Ambrose Bierce

All young people want to kick up their heels and defy convention; most of them would prefer to do it at not too heavy cost.

Elmer H. Davis

Did it ever occur to you that there is a good deal of fun in being shocked?

Edgar W. Howe

It's going to be fun to watch and see how long the meek can keep the earth after they inherit it.

Frank McKinney (Kin) Hubbard

Fun is like life insurance. The older you get, the more it costs.

Hubbard

The only good in pretending is the fun we get out of fooling ourselves that we fool somebody.

Booth Tarkington

The sound of a party is a sound of amity, of human beings who have become for the moment, and for nonaggressive reasons, something outside themselves.

Jessamyn West

Future

Every tomorrow has two handles. We can take hold of it with the handle of anxiety or the handle of faith. We should live for the future, and yet should find out life in the fidelities of the present; the last is only the method of the first.

Henry Ward Beecher

We steal if we touch tomorrow. It is God's.

Beecher

Future: That period of time in which our affairs prosper, our friends are true, and our happiness is assured.

Ambrose Bierce

Omen: A sign that something will happen if nothing happens.

Bierce

Prophecy: The art and practice of selling one's credibility for future delivery.

Bierce

The geographic frontier in America is gone. No longer can a young man "go west" and stake out his claim. But the scientific frontier in America is barely scratched. And the scientific frontier has no limit. It is limited only by the mind and the imagination of man. Its horizons are vertical, not horizontal.

Earl L. Butz

With high hope for the future, no prediction is ventured.

Abraham Lincoln

The best thing about the future is that it comes only one day at a time.

Lincoln

The future will be better tomorrow.

Danforth Quayle

Games

Gambling with cards or dice, or stocks, is all one thing; it is getting money without giving an equivalent for it.

Henry Ward Beecher

True luck consists not in holding the best of the cards at the table: luckiest he who knows just when to rise and go home.

John Milton Hay

I say banish bridge; let's find some pleasanter way of being miserable together.

Don Herold

Down home there was only one player in the pinochle parlor who knew how to shuffle. Unless you sat at his table, you'd keep getting the same cards back.

Herb Shriner

Generosity

Bounty: The liberality of one who has much, in permitting one who has nothing to get all that he can.

Ambrose Bierce

God

Theology is science of mind applied to God.

Henry Ward Beecher

God washes the eyes by tears until they can behold the invisible land where tears shall come no more.

Beecher

God pardons like a mother who kisses away the repentant tears of a child.

Beecher

We are always in the forge, or on the anvil; by trials God is shaping us for higher things.

Beecher

God rains his goodness and mercy as widespread as the dew, and if we lack them, it is because we will not open our hearts to receive them.

Beecher

God has marked the American people as his chosen nation to finally lead in the regeneration of the world.

Albert J. Beveridge

Take not God's name in vain; select a time when it will have effect.

Ambrose Bierce

Impiety: Your irreverence toward my deity.

Bierce

House of God: A building with a steeple and a mortgage on it.

Bierce

Piety: Reverence for the Supreme Being based upon his supposed resemblance to man.

Bierce

God will save the good American, and seat him at his right hand on the golden throne.

Theodore Dreiser

What hath God wrought?

Annie Ellsworth

What do you suppose God thinks of a man (created in his own image) putting on his pants in an upper berth?

Don Herold

We hear a great deal about the Lord loving cheerful givers; we wonder where he finds them.

Edgar W. Howe

We love the Lord, of course, but we often wonder what He finds to love in us. —Howe

We trust, sir, that God is on our side. It is more important to know that we are on God's side.

Abraham Lincoln

I can see how it might be possible for a man to look down upon the Earth and be an atheist, but I cannot conceive how he could look up into the heavens and say there is no God.

Lincoln

Without the assistance of the Divine Being . . . I cannot succeed. With that assistance, I cannot fail.

Lincoln

The Almighty has his own purposes.

Lincoln

When the consensus of scholarship says one thing and the word of God another, the consensus of scholarship can go plumb to hell for all I care.

William Ashley (Billy) Sunday

Gossip

She told him it was terrible to hear such things as he told her and to please go ahead.

George Ade

Rumor: A favorite weapon of the assassins of character.

Ambrose Bierce

Half the evil in the world is gossip started by good people.

Edgar W. Howe

When a man tells you what people are saying about you, tell him what people are saying about him—that will immediately take his mind off your troubles.

Howe

Gossip: Vice enjoyed vicariously—the sweet, subtle satisfaction without the risk.

Frank McKinney (Kin) Hubbard

When a woman says, "I don't wish to mention any names," it isn't necessary.

Hubbard

When some folks don't know nothing mean about someone, they switch the subject.

Hubbard

Conversation is when three women stand on the corner talking. Gossip is when one of them leaves.

Herb Shriner

Government

It usually takes a hundred years to make a law, then, after the law has done its work, it usually takes another hundred years to get rid of it.

Henry Ward Beecher

It is for men to choose whether they will govern themselves or be governed.

Beecher

The worse thing in the world, next to anarchy, is government.

Beecher

Life represents the efforts of men to organize society; government, the efforts of selfishness to overthrow liberty.

Beecher

Senate: A body of elderly gentlemen charged with duties and misdemeanors.

Ambrose Bierce

Congress: A body of men who meet to repeal laws.

Bierce

Administration: An ingenious abstraction in politics, designed to receive the kicks and cuffs due to the premier or president.

Bierce

Absolute: Independent, irresponsible. An absolute monarchy is one in which the sovereign does as he pleases so long as he pleases the assassins. Not many absolute monarchies are left, most of them having been replaced by limited monarchies, where the sovereign's power for evil (and for good) is greatly curtailed, and by republics, which are governed by chance.

Bierce

Insurrection: Disaffection's failure to substitute misrule for bad government.

Bierce

God, I knew it [state government] was big, but I didn't think it was this big. It goes on forever. You think you've seen it all, and then you turn the corner and there's another big hunk of it.

Roger Branigin

There is nothing in our government [the ballot] cannot remove or amend.

Eugene V. Debs

I admit to being opposed to the present form of government: I admit being opposed to the present social system. I am doing what little I can to do away with the rule of the great body of people by a relatively small class and establish in this country industrial and social democracy.

Debs

The government has ceased to function . . . the corporations are the government.

Theodore Dreiser

Properly conceived, the Constitution is not a burden in the making of policy, but a source of strength because it specifies a process for making policy through informed consent.

Lee H. Hamilton

The only legitimate right to govern is an express grant of power from the governed.

William Henry Harrison

I believe and I say it is true Democratic feeling, that all the measures of the government are directed to the purpose of making the rich richer and the poor poorer.

Harrison

See to the government. See that the government does not acquire too much power. Keep a check upon your rulers. Do this, and liberty is safe.

Harrison

We admit of no government by divine right, believing that so far as power is concerned the Beneficent Creator has made no distinction amongst men.

Harrison

A decent and manly examination of the acts of government should be not only tolerated, but encouraged.

Harrison

If by . . . strong government . . . one without responsibility is intended, which may put men to death, and immure them in dungeons, without trial, and one where the army is everything, and the people nothing, I must say, that . . . the wildest anarchy would be preferable.

Harrison

The delicate duty of devising schemes of revenue should be left where the Constitution has placed it—with the immediate representatives of the people.

Harrison

The government is mainly an expensive organization to regulate evildoers and tax those who behave: government does little for fairly respectable people except annoy them.

Edgar W. Howe

Gentlemen talk of government by the people, for the people, etc. There never was any such government; that was one of Abe Lincoln's jokes.

Howe

If the government was as afraid of disturbing the consumer as it is of disturbing business, this would be some democracy.

Frank McKinney (Kin) Hubbard

I don't look for much to come out of government ownership as long as we have Democrats and Republicans.

Hubbard

What is conservatism? Is it not adherence to the old and tried, against the new and untried?

Abraham Lincoln

No man is good enough to govern another man without the other's consent.

Lincoln

While the people retain their virtue and vigilance, no administration, by any extreme of wickedness or folly, can very seriously injure the government in the short space of four years.

Lincoln

I have been selected to fill an important office for a brief period, and am now, in your eyes, invested with an influence which will soon pass away; but should my administration prove to be a very wicked one, or what is more probable, a very foolish one, if you, the people, are true to yourselves and the Constitution, there is but little harm that I can do, thank God.

Lincoln

Must a government of necessity be too strong for the liberties of its people or too weak to maintain its own existence?

Lincoln

The legitimate object of government is to do for a community of people, whatever they need to have done, but cannot do at all, or cannot so well do for themselves, in their separate and individual capacities.

Lincoln

I desire to so conduct the affairs of this administration that if, at the end . . . I have lost every friend on Earth, I shall have one friend left, and that friend shall be down inside me.

Lincoln

It is safe to assert that no government proper ever had a provision in its organic law for its own termination.—Lincoln

Any people anywhere, being inclined and having the power, have the right to rise up and shake off the existing government and form a new one. This is a most valuable and sacred right—a right which we hope and believe is to liberate the world.

Lincoln

That government of the people, by the people, for the people, shall not perish from the Earth.

Lincoln

I go for all sharing the privileges of the government who assist in bearing its burdens. Consequently I go for admitting all whites to the right of suffrage who pay taxes or bear arms (by no means excluding females).

Lincoln

The trouble with America today is there are too many preachers legislating and too few legislators praying.

Thomas R. Marshall

It's got so it is as easy to amend the Constitution of the United States as it used to be to draw a cork.

Marshall

The way the government interfered with private business is enough to drive a fellow crazy. That old government moved into Tennessee and bought a lot of hilly land. Then they signed a proclamation making this land into the Great Smoky Mountain National Park, and thereby ruined the finest settlement of moonshiners in the USA.

Ernie Pyle

Looks like Congress was right smart about the new taxes. They put a big tax on liquor, then they raised all the other taxes so as to drive people to drink.

Herb Shriner

We would be a lot safer if the government would take its money out of science and put it into astrology and the reading of palms . . . only in superstition is there hope. If you want to become a friend of civilization, then become an enemy of the truth and a fanatic for harmless balderdash.

Kurt Vonnegut

The Constitution does not provide for first- and second-class citizens.

Wendell L. Willkie

Today it is not big business that we have to fear. It is big government.

Willkie

Guests

Hospitality: The virtue that induces us to feed and lodge certain persons who are not in need of food and lodging.

Ambrose Bierce

Better late than before anybody has invited you.

Bierce

To be an ideal guest, stay at home.

Edgar W. Howe

Nobody can be as agreeable as an uninvited guest.

Frank McKinney (Kin) Hubbard

There's no way to recondition a welcome when it's worn out.

Hubbard

The guest who has to be drugged with alcohol to make him interesting is hardly worth inviting in the first place.

Roy Smith

Guilt

Indiscretion: The guilt of woman.

Ambrose Bierce

I should have been put in jail for my political activities, but I am not guilty of murder.

David Curtis (D. C.) Stephenson

Happiness

Do not look back on happiness or dream of it in the future. You are only sure of today; do not let yourself be cheated out of it.

Henry Ward Beecher

Happiness is not the end of life; character is.

Beecher

Happiness: An agreeable sensation arising from contemplating the misery of another.

Ambrose Bierce

Pleasure: The least hateful form of dejection.

Bierce

A lot of people these days want to hitchhike their way to utopia.

Don Herold

Science can make man comfortable, but only wisdom can make man happy.

Theodore Hesburgh

It's pretty hard to tell what does bring happiness; poverty and wealth have both failed.

Frank McKinney (Kin) Hubbard

Where ignorance is bliss, it's foolish to borrow your neighbor's newspaper.

Hubbard

Happiness is the goal of every normal human being.

George Jean Nathan

What have I got out of life? Happiness for the most part and an income that has pleased me.

Cole Porter

You're as happy as you allow yourself to be—so why be unhappy?

Marilyn Quayle

The world is full of happy people, but no one ever hears of them. You have to fight and make a scandal to get into the paper.

Gene Stratton-Porter

So long as we can lose any happiness, we possess some. —Booth Tarkington

Cherish all your happy moments: they make a fine cushion for old age.

Tarkington

The only way to happiness is never to give happiness a thought.

David Elton Trueblood

In spite of chain smoking Pall Malls since I was fourteen, I think my wind is still good enough for me to go chasing after happiness.

Kurt Vonnegut

Human beings will be happier—not when they cure cancer or get to Mars or eliminate racial prejudice or flush Lake Erie but when they find ways to inhabit primitive communities again. That's my utopia.

Vonnegut

Happiness must be achieved through liberty rather than in spite of liberty.

Wendell L. Willkie

Harm

Injury: An offense next in degree of enormity to a slight.

Ambrose Bierce

It only hurt once, from the beginning to end.

James (Doc) Counsilman
on crossing the
English Channel at age fifty-eight

Hate

Hate is a corrosive poison that eats into the soul. You can't afford to hate anybody.

Bruce Calvert

Hate I consider is an internal sin. And hate is closely associated with fear. I think fear breeds defeatism, and that is a disease that we cannot afford in this country if we're going to maintain our position in the family of freedom-loving people.

David M. Shoup

Hatred is like vitamins, you do feel better.

Kurt Vonnegut

Health

This could very well become one of the worst health problems in the history of the world.

Otis R. Bowen
on AIDS

Thousands upon thousands of persons have studied disease. Almost no one has studied health.

Adelle Davis

As I see it, every day you do one of two things: build health or produce disease in yourself.

Davis

Nutrition is a young subject; it has been kicked around like a puppy that cannot take care of itself. Food faddists and crackpots have kicked it pretty cruelly. . . . They seem to believe that unless food tastes like Socratic hemlock, it cannot build health. Frankly, I often wonder what such persons plan to do with good health in case they acquire it.

Davis

If this country is to survive, the best-fed nation myth had better be recognized for what it is; propaganda designed to produce wealth but not health.

Davis

It is strange indeed that the more we learn about how to build health, the less healthy Americans become.

Davis

In every case, vitamin C appears to be the good Christian ready to soothe the aching brow.

Davis

Two things are bad for the heart—running uphill and running down people.

Bernard F. Gimbel

There is only one thing people like that is good for them: a good night's sleep.

Edgar W. Howe

A bad cold wouldn't be so annoying if it weren't for the advice of our friends.

Frank McKinney (Kin) Hubbard

Like everybody else, when I don't know what else to do, I seem to go in for catching cold.

George Jean Nathan

I get plenty of exercise carrying the coffins of my friends who exercise.

Red Skelton

We are healthy only to the extent that our ideas are humane.

Kurt Vonnegut

Hell

A clergyman writes us that we are a child of the devil. We hope our brother will forgive us.

Ambrose Bierce

The road to hell is thick with taxicabs.

Don Herold

I do not believe there is a devil, but we deserve one.

Edgar W. Howe

Let the heathen go to hell; help your neighbor.

Howe

There may be some doubt about hell beyond the grave but there is no doubt about there being one on this side of it.

Howe

There never was a devil who didn't advise people to keep out of hell.

Howe

Hell is a place where a man is visited by a good many of his kin.

Howe

If there is no hell, a good many preachers are obtaining money under false pretenses.

William Ashley (Billy) Sunday

History

When great changes occur in history, when great principles are involved, as a rule the majority are wrong. The minority are usually right.

Henry Ward Beecher

History is not that which men do worthily, but that which they do successfully.

Beecher

Historian: A broad-gauge gossip.

Ambrose Bierce

History: An account mostly false, of events unimportant, which are brought about by rulers mostly knaves, and soldiers mostly fools.

Bierce

Prehistoric: Antedating the art and practice of perpetuating falsehood.

Bierce

History is the torch that is meant to illuminate the past to guard us against the repetition of our mistakes of other days. We cannot join in the rewriting of history to make it conform to our comfort and convenience.

Claude G. Bowers

We will hereafter believe less history than ever, now that we have seen how it is made.

Don Herold

Not until the game is over and all the chips have been counted can you calculate a man's winnings or losses and not until he stands against the perspective of history can you correctly measure his stature.

Jimmy Hoffa

The history of mankind is one long record of giving revolution another trial, and limping back at last to sanity, safety, and work.

Edgar W. Howe

Fellow citizens, we cannot escape history. We . . . will be remembered in spite of ourselves.

Abraham Lincoln

How the devil did the Indians get over that iron fence?

James Whitcomb Riley
on seeing the Tippecanoe Battlefield
Memorial site

Historians in the future, in my opinion, will congratulate us on very little other than our clowning and our jazz.

Kurt Vonnegut

Hobbies

Fishing seems to be the favorite form of loafing.

Edgar W. Howe

If an individual collects anything long enough, it will eventually have some value.

Alfred Kinsey

All you need to be a fisherman is patience and a worm.

Herb Shriner

Holidays

I don't believe I ever heard anybody say they wanted a Christmas card for Christmas.

Frank McKinney (Kin) Hubbard

Lots of Thanksgiving Days have been ruined by not carving the turkey in the kitchen.

Hubbard

Home

Be it ever so humble, there's no place like home for wearing what you like.

George Ade

The house is more covered with mortgages than with paint.

Ade

House: A hollow edifice erected for the habitation of man, rat, mouse, beetle, cockroach, fly, mosquito, flea, bacillus, and microbe.

Ambrose Bierce

Houseless: Having paid all taxes on household goods.

Bierce

Home: The place of last resort, open all night.

Bierce

Architect: One who drafts a plan of your house and plans a draft of your money.

Bierce

Very few people understand to what straits the president's family has been put at times for lack of accommodation.

Caroline Scott (Mrs. Benjamin) Harrison, 1898
commenting on the fact that the White House
had only one bathroom

Nothing is leisurely as a bathroom drainpipe.

Don Herold

What is home without a hot-water bottle?

Herold

Of all the home remedies a good wife is the best.

Frank McKinney (Kin) Hubbard

The fellow that owns his own home is always just coming out of a hardware store.

Hubbard

The fellow that brags about how cheap he heats his home always sees the first robin.

Hubbard

Lots of fellows think a home is only good to borrow money on.

Hubbard

In using a carpet sweeper with one hand and carrying the baby with the other it will be found very difficult to reach a hair-pin back of the piano.

Hubbard

The fellow that's mean around the home is always the life and sunshine of some lodge.

Hubbard

Hoosiers

Forty or fifty years ago the native son who went traveling owned up to an indefinite residence somewhere between Louisville and Chicago. Today the Hoosier abroad claims Indiana fervently, hoping to be mistaken for an author.

George Ade

Hoosier: He is a puzzling combination of shy provincial, unfettered democrat, and Fourth of July orator. He is a student by choice, a poet by sneaking inclination, and a storyteller by reason of his nativity.

Ade

Indianans have an ability to see sin at a distance but never at their very feet. Indianapolis is shocked by vice in East Chicago; Bloomington is horrified by what goes on in Terre Haute or South Bend, and so on.

Roger Branigin

I'm a Hoosier, a Baptist, and a Democrat. By God, you can't get any commoner than that.

Branigin

Being a Hoosier is just like being a boy all your life long. The years cannot put you into a cast, nor cover your natal characteristics with the thin veneer of artificiality. The Hoosier does not wait for an invitation to do a thing and then tremble at his lack of power. What he wants, he takes.

Thomas R. Marshall

It is open season the year around in Indiana for literature, learning, laws, politics, business. All Hoosiers are mighty hunters and the game is plentiful.

Marshall

Hoosiers are congenitally inquisitive. That means nosy, in a nice sort of way.

Herb Shriner

Hope

Hope: Desire and expectation rolled into one.

Ambrose Bierce

There is nothing so well known as that we should not expect something for nothing—but we all do and call it hope.

Edgar W. Howe

This is the year you expected so much of last year.

Howe

Every man knows better than he hopes.

Howe

Human Nature

I detest an apology. The world is full of people who are always making trouble and apologizing for it. If a man respects me, he will not give himself occasion for apology. An offense cannot be wiped out in that way. If it could, we would substitute apologies for hangings. I hope you will never apologize to me; I should regard it as evidence that you had wronged me.

Edgar W. Howe

To err is human, but to admit it isn't.

Frank McKinney (Kin) Hubbard

Human action can be modified to some extent, but human nature cannot be changed.

Abraham Lincoln

Human nature will not change. In any future great national trial, compared with the men of this, we shall have as weak and as strong, as silly and as wise, as bad and as good.

Lincoln

With the catching ends the pleasures of the chase.

Lincoln

Humor

A person without a sense of humor is like a wagon without springs, jolted by every pebble in the road.

Henry Ward Beecher

Humorist: A plague that would have softened down the hoary austerity of Pharaoh's heart and persuaded him to dismiss Israel with his best wishes, cat-quick.

Ambrose Bierce

A humorist is a man who feels bad but who feels good about it.

Don Herold

Humor endows us with the capacity to clarify the obscure, to simplify the complex, to deflate the pompous, to chastise the arrogant, to point a moral, and to adorn a tale.

John T. McCutcheon

Humor is truth in an intoxicated condition.

George Jean Nathan

Humor is as personal as sex.

Jean Shepherd

When a man cannot see the humorous phases of human life or take advantage of them either in private conversation or public speech to impress some point of his own, well, in my judgment, he is most unfortunately constituted.

James E. Watson

Husbands

Married men live longer than single men, or at least they complain more about it.

Don Herold

There seems to be something about being a good dutiful husband that causes him to tow in.

Frank McKinney (Kin) Hubbard

I can always tell a fellow who has married a good housekeeper by the way he brightens up when I speak kindly of him.

Hubbard

The husband who has to get his breakfast downtown is liable to be late for dinner.

Hubbard

Ideals

When young men are beginning life, the most important period, it is often said, is that in which their habits are formed. That is a very important period. But the period in which the ideas of the young are formed and adopted is more important still. For the ideal with which you go forward to measure things determines the nature, so far as you are concerned, of everything you meet.

Henry Ward Beecher

Living up to ideals is like doing everyday work with your Sunday clothes on.

Edgar W. Howe

Some people never have anything except ideals.

Howe

Illness

He felt like the symptoms on a medicine bottle.

George Ade

Distress: A disease incurred by exposure to the prosperity of a friend.

Ambrose Bierce

Before the advent of the radio, there were advantages in being a shut-in.

Don Herold

Everyone has something ancestral, even if it is nothing more than a disease.

Edgar W. Howe

I wish it were possible to pull a cold, like an aching tooth.

Howe

Independence

I think the authors of that notable instrument [Declaration of Independence] intended to include all men, but they did not intend to declare all men equal in all respects. They did not mean to say all men were equal in color, size, intellect, moral developments, or social capacity. They defined with tolerable distinctness in what respects they did consider all men created equal—equal with "certain unalienable rights among which are life, liberty and the pursuit of happiness." This they said and this they meant.

Abraham Lincoln

The assertion that "all men are created equal" was of no practical use in effecting our separation from Great Britain and it was placed in the Declaration not for that, but for future use. Its authors meant it to be—as thank God, it is now proving itself—a stumbling block to all those who in aftertimes might seek to turn a free people back into the hateful paths of despotism.

Lincoln

Wise statesmen as they were, they knew the tendency of posterity to breed tyrants: and so they established these great self-evident truths, that when in the distant future, some man, some faction, some interest, should set up the doctrine that none but rich men or none but white men, or none but Anglo-Saxons, were entitled to life, liberty, and the pursuit of happiness, their posterity might look up again to the Declaration of Independence, and take courage to renew the battle that their fathers began.

Lincoln

I have often inquired of myself, what great principle or idea it was that kept this confederacy so long together. It was not the mere matter of the separation of the colonies from the motherland; but something in that Declaration giving liberty, not alone to the people of this country, but hope to the world for all future time. It was that which gave promise that in due time the weights should be lifted from the shoulders of all man, and that all should have an equal chance. This is the sentiment embodied in that Declaration of Independence.

Lincoln

Indiana

Indiana was settled by pioneers who had the enterprise to seek new fields and the gumption to unpack and settle down when they found themselves in the promised land.

George Ade

Many good men come from Indiana: the better they are the quicker they come. —Ade

Indiana grows all the crops and propaganda known to the temperate zone.

Ade

I'm in no hurry to return to Indiana. I haven't a thing to do when I get there.

John Dillinger
after his arrest in Arizona

This is a most peculiar state. It may not be so dynamic nor yet so creative, sociologically, as it is fecund of things that relate to the spirit—or perhaps I had better say to poetry and the interpretative arts.

Theodore Dreiser

I insist that the Hoosier is different mentally and spiritually to the average American. He is softer, less sophisticated, more poetic. . . . He dreams a lot. He likes to play in simple ways. He is not as grasping as other Americans. . . . That may be due to the fact that he is not practical, being as poetic and good-natured as he is. . . . In a crude way, perhaps, he has the temperament of the artist.

Dreiser

It seems to me that, if anything, the state is a little bit sluggish, intellectually and otherwise. Or, if it isn't that, exactly, then certainly there is an element of self-complacency that permits the largest percentage of its population to rest content in the most retarding forms of political, religious, and social folderol.

Dreiser

There is about [Indiana] a charm I shall not be able to express. . . . This is a region not unlike those which produce gold or fleet horses, or oranges or adventurers.

Dreiser

I do not know whether it is prejudice or not, but anyway I always have a very high opinion of a state whose chief production is corn.

Benjamin Harrison

A lady from Florida who has spent some time in Canada where they have perfectly straight roads remarked that a snake would break its back traveling over our winding thoroughfares. I told her that if we straighten them out we wouldn't have room for all of them.

Frank M. Hohenberger
explaining Brown County's terrain

Yes, the old state, as the days have come and gone, has struck a right good average. It has perhaps no towering mountain peaks, but it has surely furnished as many first-grade second-class men in every department of life as any state in the Union.

Thomas R. Marshall

This Indiana idea, this conception of the state as a bucolic place inhabited by pleasant, simple, neighborly folks, contains a good deal of mythology. Hoosiers today try to conform to the myth.

John Bartlow Martin

All northern and central Indiana is as flat as a board. Neat farms checker it, and the roads are straight as a ruler. Big barns and regular fences and waving fields of grain splash across the endless landscape. But some thirty miles south of Indianapolis the land begins to undulate, the hills are covered thick with forest, the roads wind, and the fields become patches on slopes. It is hill country because this is where the great glacier stopped and melted away and left its giant rubble piled.

Ernie Pyle

You can tell I'm an Indiana boy. There's something about a fellow from Indiana. I don't know what it is. Well . . . I do know what it is, but I don't like to think about it.

Herb Shriner

THE INDIANA BOOK OF QUOTES

I myself grew up in Indianapolis, Indiana, where common speech sounds like a band saw cutting galvanized tin and employs a vocabulary as unornamental as a monkey wrench.

Kurt Vonnegut

I am by all I know a Californian, and by all I imagine, a Hoosier.

Jessamyn West

Influence

The blossom cannot tell what becomes of its odor, and no man can tell what becomes of his influence and example, that roll away from him, and go beyond his ken on their perilous mission.

Henry Ward Beecher

Insults

We have a full quota of smart alecks, but not one serf.

George Ade

I knew her when she didn't know where her next husband was coming from.

Anne Baxter

The ignorant classes are the dangerous classes. Ignorance is the womb of monsters.

Henry Ward Beecher

His mind works in the right direction but seldom works clearly and cleanly. His bread is of unbolted flour, and bush straw, too, mixed in the bran, and sometimes gravel stones.

*Beecher, referring
to Abraham Lincoln*

Backbite: To speak of a man as you find him when he can't find you.

Ambrose Bierce

The sovereign of insufferables.

*Bierce
on writer Oscar Wilde*

He couldn't keep track of an elephant in ten feet of snow.

Roger Branigin

The use of proverbs is characteristic of an unlettered people. They are invaluable treasures to dunces with good memories.

John Milton Hay

A half baked glib little briefless jackleg lawyer, grasping with anxiety to collar that $50,000 salary, promised the millennium to everybody with a hole in his pants and destruction to everybody with a clean shirt.

*Hay
on William Jennings Bryan*

LBJ [Lyndon Baines Johnson] always referred to Robert Kennedy in one way. He called him "the little shit." I'll buy that in spades although in that connection I wouldn't have called him "little."

Jimmy Hoffa

I hope the worms eat his eyes out.

*Hoffa, on hearing of
Robert Kennedy's assassination*

General [George] Marshall is not only willing, he is eager to play the role of a front man for traitors. The truth is this is no new role for him, for General George C. Marshall is a living lie ... unless he himself was desperate, he could not possibly agree to continue as an errand boy, a front man, a stooge, or a co-conspirator for this administration's crazy assortment of collectivists, cutthroat crackpots and Communist fellow-traveling appeasers.

*William E. Jenner, opposing Marshall's
nomination for secretary of state*

He is only a filthy-brained child, conceived in ruthlessness, and dedicated to the proposition that Judas Iscariot was a piker.

*Jenner
referring to Drew Pearson*

He can compress the most words into the smallest ideas better than any man I ever met.
Abraham Lincoln

THE INDIANA BOOK OF QUOTES

I did keep a grocery, and I did sell cotton, candles, and cigars and sometimes whiskey; but I remember in those days Mr. [Stephen] Douglas was one of my best customers. Many a time I have stood on one side of the counter and sold whiskey to Mr. Douglas on the other side, but the difference between us now is: I have left my side of the counter, but Mr. Douglas still sticks to his tenaciously as ever.

Lincoln

His argument [Stephen Douglas's] is as thin as the homeopathic soup that was made by boiling the shadow of a pigeon that had been starved to death.

Lincoln

The Queen of the Nile.

George Jean Nathan, referring to Tallulah Bankhead

I am disappointed in my continued disappointment in Williams. And I am afraid I am doomed to keep being disappointed in him until either I enter my second childhood or he outgrows his.

Nathan, referring to Tennessee Williams

Want to hear a sad story about the [Michael] Dukakis campaign? The governor of Massachusetts, he lost his top naval adviser last week. The rubber duck drowned in his bathtub.

Danford Quayle

Liberalism's sensitive philosopher king.

Quayle on Governor Mario Cuomo

Intelligence

Intelligence is making the noblest and best in our curious heritage prevail.

Charles A. Beard

Brain: An apparatus with which we think that we think.

Ambrose Bierce

These are the prerogatives of genius: to know without having learned; to draw just conclusions from unknown premises; to discern the soul of things.

Bierce

One of the strongest characteristics of genius is the power of lighting its own fire.

John Watson Foster

The brighter you are, the more you have to learn.

Don Herold

Yes, I'm optimistic; maybe in a million years people will be as intelligent as horses.

Herold

Genius is an infinite capacity for giving pains.

Herold

It takes a lot of things to prove you are smart, but only one thing to prove you are ignorant.

Herold

Thought itself is probably a superstition.

Herold

No man is smart enough to be funny when he is drunk.

Edgar W. Howe

Some folks never begin to figure till there's nothing to add.

Frank McKinney (Kin) Hubbard

Intelligent people are always on the unpopular side of anything.

Hubbard

It's what a fellow thinks he knows that hurts him.

Hubbard

Some fellows are just naturally intelligent and others have long flowing whiskers.

Hubbard

Towering genius disdains a beaten path. It seeks regions hitherto unexplored.

Abraham Lincoln

To lack intelligence is to be in the ring blindfolded.

David M. Shoup

There was a fellow down home who wasn't too bright as a kid. When they gave him those intelligence tests in school, he'd always try to put the square peg in the round holes. Funny thing is, he could do it—he was stronger than most kids.

Herb Shriner

It is exceedingly probable that there is other life in the universe more intelligent than ours.

Harold C. Urey

I was taught that the human brain was the crowning glory of evolution so far, but I think it's a very poor scheme for survival.

Kurt Vonnegut

It's what you learn after you know it all that counts.

John Wooden

International Events

International arbitration may be defined as the substitution of many burning questions for a smoldering one.

Ambrose Bierce

Immigrant: An unenlightened person who thinks one country better than another.

Bierce

Alien: An American sovereign in his probationary state.

Bierce

There is an irreversible trend to freedom and democracy in eastern Europe. But this may change.

Danford Quayle

We expect [the Salvadorans] to work toward the elimination of human rights.

Quayle

Inventions

A tool is but the extension of a man's hand, and a machine is but a complex tool. And he that invents a machine augments the power of a man and the well-being of mankind.

Henry Ward Beecher

Inventor: A person who makes an ingenious arrangement of wheels, levers, and springs, and believes it civilization.

Ambrose Bierce

Telephone: An invention of the devil that abrogates some of the advantages of making a disagreeable person keep his distance.

Bierce

It means to me what the phonograph means to Edison and the steamboat to Fulton. The Haynes car is my life.

Elwood Haynes

Back home the community's wealthiest citizen got rich after he invented a dog food that tasted like a postman's leg.

Herb Shriner

Irony

The fellow that sets on a store box with his mouth full of scrap tobacco while his wife is at home sewing for a living knows just exactly how to regulate the railroads.

Frank McKinney (Kin) Hubbard

Jail

They cannot put the Socialist movement in jail.

Eugene V. Debs

A jail is just like a nut with a worm in it. The worm can always get out.

John Dillinger

I won't cause you any trouble except to escape. —Dillinger

I can tell you this on a stack of Bibles: prisons are archaic, brutal, unregenerative, overcrowded hellholes where the inmates are treated like animals with absolutely not one humane thought given to what they are going to do once they are released. You're an animal in a cage and you're treated like one.

Jimmy Hoffa

Jobs

Fellow who runs the fix-it shop has to sleep there. The lock on the front door is busted.

Herb Shriner

Justice

Justice: A commodity that in a more or less adulterated condition the state sells to the citizen as a reward for his allegiance, taxes and personal service.

Ambrose Bierce

Amnesty: The state's magnanimity to those offenders whom it would be too expensive to punish.

Bierce

Justice is always the same, whether it be due from one man to a million, or from a million to one man.

John Milton Hay

When a man tries himself, the verdict is usually in his favor.

Edgar W. Howe

Why should there not be a patient confidence in the ultimate justice of the people? Is there any better or equal hope in the world?

Abraham Lincoln

The severest justice may not always be the best policy.

Lincoln

I have always found that mercy bears richer fruits than strict justice.

Lincoln

Knowledge

Many men are stored full of unused knowledge. . . . They are stuffed with useless ammunition.

Henry Ward Beecher

Precise knowledge is the only true knowledge, and he who does not teach exactly, does not teach at all.

Beecher

To know that one has a secret is to know half of the secret itself.

Beecher

To the small part of ignorance that we arrange and classify we give the name knowledge.

Ambrose Bierce

Wisdom is a special knowledge in excess of all that is known.

Bierce

Ignoramus: A person unacquainted with certain kinds of knowledge familiar to yourself, and having certain other kinds that you know nothing about.

Bierce

Connoisseur: A specialist who knows everything about something and nothing about anything else.

Bierce

There are two kinds of stones, as everyone knows, one of which rolls.

Amelia Earhart

When we know as much about people as hog specialists know about hogs, we'll be better off.

Lewis B. Hershey

I very early realized I wasn't good enough to play [basketball] after graduation, so I'd better figure out something I could do.

Robert Montgomery (Bobby) Knight

What we know about things that we know nothing about is the most remarkable part of our mental equipment and our education. The less we know the surer we are of our conclusions.

Thomas R. Marshall

As Mark Twain once said, "You should never trust a man who has only one way to spell a word."

Danford Quayle

We know nothing important. In the essentials we are still as wholly a mystery to ourselves as Adam was to himself.

Booth Tarkington

Labor

The prosecution of modern wars rests completely upon the operation of labor in mines, mills, and factories, so that labor fights there just as truly as the soldiers do in the trenches.

Mary Ritter Beard

No strike has ever been lost.

Eugene V. Debs

You have got to unite in the same labor union and in the same political party and *strike and vote together*, and the hour that you do that the world is yours.

Debs

There can be no defeat for the labor movement.

Debs

I know the trials and woes of workingmen, and I have always felt for them. I know that in almost every case of strikes, the men have a just cause for complaint.

Abraham Lincoln

In the early days of the world, the Almighty said to the first of our race, "In the sweat of thy face shalt thou eat bread"; and since then, if we except the light and the air of heaven, no good thing has been, or can be enjoyed by us, without having first cost labor.

Lincoln

Land

These lands are ours. No one has a right to remove us, because we were the first owners. The Great Spirit above has appointed this place for our use.

Tecumseh

Language

Slang: The speech of him who robs the literary garbage carts on their way to the dumps.

Ambrose Bierce

Language: The music with which we charm the serpents guarding another's treasure.

Bierce

Slang is that which fixes into portable shape the nebulous ideas of the vulgar.

John Milton Hay

Laughter

Mirthfulness is in the mind and you cannot get it out. It is just as good in its place as conscience or veneration.

Henry Ward Beecher

A man without mirth is like a wagon without springs, in which one is caused disagreeably to jolt by every pebble over which it turns.

Beecher

Laughter: An interior convulsion, producing a distortion of the features and accompanied by inarticulate noises. It is infectious and, though intermittent, incurable. Liability to attacks of laughter is one of the characteristics distinguishing man from the animals.

Ambrose Bierce

If you don't learn to laugh at trouble, you won't have anything to laugh at when you're old.

Edgar W. Howe

Laughter is the first thing that ages a woman. It is a smile that burst.

George Jean Nathan

Law

Laws are not masters but servants, and he rules them who obeys them.

Henry Ward Beecher

Lawful: Compatible with the will of a judge having jurisdiction.

Ambrose Bierce

Lawyer: One skilled in circumvention of the law.

Bierce

Habeas corpus: A writ by which a man may be taken out of jail when confined for the wrong crime.

Bierce

Litigant: A person about to give up his skin for the hope of retaining his bones.

Bierce

Lawsuit: A machine which you go into as a pig and come out as a sausage.

Bierce

Court fool: The plaintiff.

Bierce

Oath: In law, a solemn appeal to the Deity, made binding upon the conscience by a penalty for perjury.

Bierce

Homicide: The slaying of one human being by another. There are four kinds of homicide: felonious, excusable, justifiable, and praiseworthy, but it makes no great difference to the person slain whether he fell by one kind or another—the classification is for advantage of the lawyers.

Bierce

The court of final resort is the people, and that court will be heard from in due time.

—Eugene V. Debs

It is the government that should ask me for a pardon.

Debs, 1921
on being freed
from prison

No good cause can be promoted upon the lines of lawlessness. Mobs do not discriminate and the punishments inflicted by them have no repressive or salutary influence.

Benjamin Harrison

To the law we bow with reverence. It is the one king that commands our allegiance. We will change our king when his rule is oppressive.

Harrison

No law of man can by decree or judgment say that what is wrong in the eyes of God suddenly becomes right.

Theodore Hesburgh

Nearly every lawsuit is an insult to the intelligence of both plaintiff and defendant.

Edgar W. Howe

There are few grave legal questions involved in a poor estate.

Howe

A man must not think he can save himself the trouble of being a sensible man and a gentleman by going to his lawyer, any more than he can get himself a sound constitution by going to his doctor.

Howe

When half the men become fond of doing a thing, the other half prohibit it by law.

Howe

Every once in a while you meet a fellow in some honorable walk of life that was once admitted to the bar.

Frank McKinney (Kin) Hubbard

The only time some fellows are ever seen with their wives is after they've been indicted.

Hubbard

The constable has three sons, two self-sustaining and one employed by the city.

Hubbard

Discourage litigation. Persuade your neighbors to compromise whenever you can. . . . As a peacemaker the lawyer has a superior opportunity of being a good man. There will still be business enough.

Abraham Lincoln

A jury too frequently has at least one member more ready to hang the panel than hang the traitor.

Lincoln

There is no grievance that is a fit object of redress by mob law.

Lincoln

Let me not be understood as saying that there are no bad laws, or that grievances may not arise for the redress of which no legal provisions have been made. I mean to say no such thing. But I do mean to say that although bad laws, if they exist, should be repealed as soon as possible, still, while they continue in force, for the sake of example they should be religiously observed.

Lincoln

The best way to get a bad law repealed is to enforce it strictly.

Lincoln

It is far better to have less learning and more moral character in the practice of the law than it is to have great learning and no morals.

Thomas R. Marshall

You can't measure achievement in cleaning up the environment by the number of lawsuits filed.

William D. Ruckelshaus

I am the law in Indiana.

David Curtis (D. C.) Stephenson

Lawyers' work required sharp brains, strong vocal chords, and an iron butt.

Jessamyn West

Learning

A mother's heart is the child's schoolroom.

Henry Ward Beecher

Learning: The kind of ignorance distinguishing the studious.

Ambrose Bierce

With my mother's smile did I suck in the principles upon which the Declaration of Independence was founded.

William Henry Harrison

It seems like one of the hardest lessons to be learned in this life is where your business ends and somebody else's begins.

Frank McKinney (Kin) Hubbard

The only regret I have was that I didn't study Latin harder in school so I could converse with those people.

Danford Quayle
on visit to Latin America

Beware of the man who works hard to learn something, learns it, then finds himself no wiser than before.

Kurt Vonnegut

I had no instruction in reading. It came naturally, as if I had known all along and simply had to be told when to begin.

Dan Wakefield

Teaching is the royal road to learning.

Jessamyn West

Lies

There is no such thing as white lies; a lie is as black as a coal pit, and twice as foul.

Henry Ward Beecher

Even a liar tells a hundred truths to one lie; he has to, to make the lie good for anything.

Beecher

One whose falsehoods no longer deceive has forfeited the right to tell the truth.

Ambrose Bierce

Defame: To lie about another. To tell the truth about another.

Bierce

Fib: A lie that has not cut its teeth.

Bierce

Liar: A lawyer with a roving commission.

Bierce

Here lies Frank Pixley—as usual.

Bierce
said of a man
who had fired Bierce

Americans detest all lies except lies spoken in public or printed lies.

Edgar W. Howe

The first one to catch a circus in a lie is a boy.

Frank McKinney (Kin) Hubbard

No man has a good enough memory to make a successful liar.

Abraham Lincoln

People need good lies. There are too many bad ones.

Kurt Vonnegut

Life

Life is a series of relapses and recoveries.

George Ade

I am convinced that the world is not a mere bog in which men and women trample themselves in the mire and die. Something magnificent is taking place here amid the cruelties and tragedies, and the supreme challenge to intelligence is that of making the noblest and best in our curious heritage prevail.

Charles A. Beard

All higher motives, ideals, conceptions, sentiments in a man are no account if they do not come forward to strengthen him for the better discharge of the duties which devolve upon him in the ordinary affairs of life.

Henry Ward Beecher

We sleep, but the loom of life never stops and the pattern which was weaving when the sun went down is weaving when it comes up tomorrow.

Beecher

God asks no man whether he will accept life. This is not the choice. You must take it. The only question is how.

Beecher

No matter what looms ahead, if you can eat today, enjoy the sunlight today, mix good cheer with friends today, enjoy it and bless God for it.

Beecher

Do not look back on happiness or dream of it in the future. You are only sure of today; do not let yourself be cheated out of it.

Beecher

Let him who would wish to duplicate his every experience prate of the value of life.

Ambrose Bierce

Life: A spiritual pickle preserving the body from decay.

Bierce

Diary: A daily record of that part of one's life that he can relate to himself without blushing.

Bierce

Birth: The first and direst of all disasters.

Bierce

Humanity is suffering from its overhead charges. Life must be simplified. We must throw overboard our junk or we'll never make port.

Bruce Calvert

The effect of having other interests beyond those domestic works well. The more one does and sees and feels, the more one is able to do, and the more genuine may be one's appreciation of fundamental things like home, and love, and understanding companionship.

Amelia Earhart

Great lives never go out. They go on.

Benjamin Harrison

It is a good thing that life is not as serious as it seems to a waiter.

Don Herold

Interruptions are the spice of life.

Herold

Life goes from diapers to dignity to decomposition.

Herold

Life is like a game of cards. Reliability is the ace, industry the king, politeness the queen, thrift the jack. Common sense is playing to best advantage the cards you draw. And every day, as the game proceeds, you will find the ace, king, queen, jack in your hand and opportunity to use them.

Edgar W. Howe

About all some men accomplish in life is to send a son to Harvard.

Howe

So far I haven't heard of anybody who wants to stop living on account of the cost.

Frank McKinney (Kin) Hubbard

Human life and turnips remain cheap and plentiful.

Hubbard

Live so that you can at least get the benefit of the doubt.

Hubbard

Lots of folks don't know when they're well off, but ten times as many don't know when they're not well off.

Hubbard

Be a life long or short, its completeness depends on what it was lived for.

David Starr Jordan

The problem of life is not to make life easier, but to make men stronger.

Jordan

No one is really miserable who has not tried to cheapen life.

Jordan

Today is your day and mine, the only day we have, the day in which we play our part. What our part may signify in the great whole, we may not understand; but we are here to play it, and now is our time.

Jordan

My whole existence has been rather humdrum.

Eli Lilly

It is a great piece of folly to attempt to make anything out of me or my early life. It can all be condensed into a single sentence, and that sentence you will find in Gray's "Elegy": "The short and simple annals of the poor."

Abraham Lincoln

Do not worry. Eat three square meals a day, say your prayers, be courteous to your creditors, keep your digestion good, steer clear of biliousness, exercise, go slow and go easy. Maybe there are other things that your special case requires to make you happy, but, my friend, these I reckon will give you a good life.

Lincoln

This has been the law of my life: To give away gladly and joyfully to anybody who wanted it, anything I did not want myself.

Thomas R. Marshall

My code of life and conduct is simply this; work hard; play to the allowable limit; disregard equally the good and bad opinion of others; never do a friend a dirty trick . . . never grow indignant over anything . . . live the moment to the utmost of its possibilities . . . and be satisfied with life always, but never with oneself.

George Jean Nathan

Life is not a miracle. It is a natural phenomenon and can be expected to appear whenever there is a planet whose conditions duplicate those of the earth.

Harold C. Urey

You all of a sudden realize that you are being ruled by people you went to high school with. You all of a sudden catch on that life is nothing but high school— class officers, cheerleaders, and all.

Kurt Vonnegut

Life happens too fast for you ever to think about it. If you could just persuade people of this, but they insist on amassing information.

Vonnegut

Groan and forget it.

Jessamyn West

Losing

It is defeat that turns bone to flint, and gristle to muscle, and makes men invincible, and forms those heroic natures that are now in ascendancy in the world. Do not then be afraid of defeat. You are never so near to victory as when defeated in a good cause.

Henry Ward Beecher

No man is such a conqueror as the man who has defeated himself.

Beecher

It's the good loser that finally loses out.

Frank McKinney (Kin) Hubbard

The cause of civil liberty must not be surrendered at the end of one or even one hundred defeats.

Abraham Lincoln

Show me a good and gracious loser, and I'll show you a failure. —Knute Rockne

One loss is good for the soul. Too many losses are not good for the coach.

Rockne

I would rather lose in a cause that I know some day will triumph than to triumph in a cause that I know some day will fail.

Wendell L. Willkie

Love

There is no friendship, no love, like that of a parent for a child.

Henry Ward Beecher

Love cannot endure indifference. It needs to be wanted. Like a lamp, it needs to be fed out of the oil of another's heart, or its flame burns low.

Beecher

To love I must have something I can put my arms around.

Beecher

Love is more just than justice.

Beecher

Women in love are less ashamed than men. They have less to be ashamed of.

Ambrose Bierce

Love is a delightful day's journey. At the farther end kiss your companion and say farewell.

Bierce

Love: A temporary insanity curable by marriage or by removal of the patient from the influences under which he incurred the disorder. . . . A disease prevalent only among civilized races living under artificial conditions.

Bierce

Jealous: Unduly concerned about the preservation of that which can be lost only if not worth keeping.

Bierce

The gods love a cheerful grumbler.

Bruce Calvert

It is a disquieting fact (but a fact) that people are more often loved for their imperfections than for their inimitable righteousness.

Lloyd C. Douglas

Science without love will destroy the earth.

Max Ehrmann

Love is one of life's greatest gifts. To love and to be loved is to be fortified against the onslaughts of fate.

Ehrmann

The romance of love, the soul flight, that deep wonderful feeling, is as real as a brick house.

Ehrmann

Love your neighbor, but be careful of your neighborhood.

John Milton Hay

The love game is never called on account of darkness.

Don Herold

No man ever loved a woman he was afraid of.

Edgar W. Howe

I do not love my neighbor as myself, and apologize to no one. I treat my neighbor as fairly and politely as I hope to be treated, but there is no law in nature or common sense ordering me to go beyond that.

Howe

We cannot permit love to run riot; we must build fences around it, as we do around pigs.

Howe

There are so many hearts that I have always believed there should be a whole one for everybody.

Howe

Half the people who make love could be arrested for counterfeiting.

Howe

Love affairs have always greatly interested me, but I do not greatly care for them in books or moving pictures. In a love affair I wish to be the hero, with no audience present.

Howe

If there is any one thing that a man should do in private, it is his loving.

Howe

Every lover is a liar.

Howe

Love is a game in which both players always cheat.

Howe

Half the declarations of love a man makes to a woman are to quiet her suspicions.

Howe

A foolish girl may make a lover a husband, but it takes a clever woman to keep a husband a lover.

Howe

If a woman doesn't chase a man a little, she doesn't love him.

Howe

We want to knock hard on Cupid. Is it any wonder that love affairs go wrong when entrusted to a little boy so young he hasn't enough sense to put his clothes on?

Howe

You may talk all you please about patriotism and religion, but a right good love affair moves a man more than anything else.

Howe

Of course there is such a thing as love, or there wouldn't be so many divorces.

Howe

It is better to have loved and lost than never to have been sued.

Frank McKinney (Kin) Hubbard

All the world loves a lover, but not while the lovemaking is going on.

Hubbard

Love's labor is the poorest paid of all.

Hubbard

Love demands infinitely more than friendship.

George Jean Nathan

Romantic love is the privilege of emperors, kings, soldiers, and artists; it is the butt of democrats, traveling salesmen, magazine poets, and the writers of American novels.

Nathan

Love is an emotion experienced by the many and enjoyed by the few.

Nathan

Love is the emotion that a woman feels always for a poodle dog and sometimes for a man.

Nathan

If someone says "I love you" to me, I feel as though I had a pistol pointed at my head. What can anybody reply under such conditions but that which the pistol holder requires? "I love you, too."

Kurt Vonnegut

It is the loving, not the loved, woman who feels lovable.

Jessamyn West

Luck

The worse piece of luck that can happen to a busy man is to make a favorable impression on a bore.

Edgar W. Howe

Man

Man is at the bottom an animal, midway, a citizen, and at the top, divine. But the climate of this world is such that few ripen at the top.

Henry Ward Beecher

You never know till you try to reach them how accessible men are; but you must approach each man by the right door.

Beecher

Man: An animal so lost in rapturous contemplation of what he thinks he is as to overlook what he indubitably ought to be. His chief occupation is extermination of other animals and his own species, which, however, multiplies with such insistent rapidity as to infest the whole habitable earth and Canada.

Ambrose Bierce

A man is the sum of his ancestors; to reform him you must begin with a dead ape and work downward through a million graves. He is like the lower end of a suspended chain; you can sway him slightly to the right or to the left, but remove your hand and he falls into line with the other links.

Bierce

Man: A member of the unconsidered or negligible sex. . . . The genus has two varieties: good providers and bad providers.

Bierce

All modern men are descended from a wormlike creature, but it shows more on some people.

William Jacob Cuppy

Man has not yet reached his best. He never will reach his best until he walks the upward way side by side with a woman.

Eugene V. Debs

Man's superiority will be shown, not in the fact that he has enslaved his wife, but that he has made her free.

Debs

A man without decision can never be said to belong to himself.

John Watson Foster

The natural man has a difficult time getting along in this world. Half the people think he is a scoundrel because he is not a hypocrite.

Edgar W. Howe

No man would listen to you talk if he didn't know it was his turn next.

Howe

A man likes marvelous things so he invents them and is astonished.

Howe

I never knew a man so mean that I was not willing he should admire me.

Howe

If a man should suddenly be changed to a woman, he couldn't get his clothes off.

Howe

If all the people in the world should agree to sympathize with a certain man at a certain hour, they could not cure his headache.

Howe

There is always a type of man who says he loves his fellow man and expects to make a living at it.

Howe

There are so many more mean men than good that a good man is always under suspicion.

Howe

Some men are alive simply because it is against the law to kill them.

Howe

There is only one grade of men; they are all contemptible.

Howe

To err is human, but to admit it isn't.

Frank McKinney (Kin) Hubbard

Some men are born great, some achieve greatness, and others just keep still.

Hubbard

Surely God would not have created such a being as man . . . to exist only for a day! No, no, man was made for immortality.

Abraham Lincoln

It is the mark of a superior man that, left to himself, he is able endlessly to amuse, interest, and entertain himself out of his personal stock of meditations, ideas, criticism, memories, philosophy, humor, and what not.

George Jean Nathan

I have no hostility towards men. Some of my best friends are men. I married a man and my father was a man.

Jill Ruckelshaus

No one in the whole world knows all a man's bigness and all his littleness as his wife does.

Gene Stratton-Porter

A man without a home can't be lost.

Kurt Vonnegut

It strikes me as gruesome and comical that in our culture we have an expectation that a man can always solve his problems. This is so untrue that it makes me want to laugh—or cry.

Vonnegut

I can think of no more stirring symbol of man's humanity to man than a fire engine.

Vonnegut

Manners

Politeness: The most acceptable hypocrisy.

Ambrose Bierce

Everyone has to think to be polite; the first impulse is to be impolite.

Edgar W. Howe

Being a gentleman is hiding your manners.

Howe

A man should be as polite all the time as a candidate is just before election.

Howe

"It doesn't cost anything to be courteous" is an old saying, but if somebody asks you what time it is on a dark backstreet, guess at it.

Frank McKinney (Kin) Hubbard

THE INDIANA BOOK OF QUOTES

Some folks are too polite to be up to any good.

Hubbard

The test of good manners is to be able to put up pleasantly with bad ones.

Wendell L. Willkie

Marriage

Married men: Merely bachelors who weakened under the strain.

George Ade

If it were not for the presents, an elopement would be preferable.

Ade

Those who marry to escape something usually find something else.

Ade

Don't try to marry an entire family or it may work out that way.

Ade

All women marry gods, but gladly consent afterwards to live with men.

Henry Ward Beecher

Well-married, a man is winged; ill-matched, he is shackled.

Beecher

Marriage: The state or condition of a community consisting of a master, a mistress, and two slaves, making in all, two.

Ambrose Bierce

Wedding: A ceremony at which two persons undertake to become one, one undertakes to become nothing, and nothing undertakes to become supportable.

Bierce

Bigamy: A mistake in taste.

Bierce

Bride: A woman with a fine prospect of happiness behind her.

Bierce

Helpmate: The wife, or bitter half.

Bierce

A bad marriage is like an electric thrilling-machine: it makes you dance, but you can't let go.

Bierce

Divorce: A resumption of diplomatic relations and rectification of boundaries.

Bierce

Incompatibility: In matrimony, a similarity of tastes, particularly the taste for domination.

Bierce

Caesar might have married Cleopatra, but he had a wife at home—there's always something.

William Jacob Cuppy

Henry VIII had so many wives because his dynastic sense was very strong whenever he saw a maid of honor.

Cuppy

Ours is a reasonable and contented partnership, my husband with his solo jobs and I with mine; but the system of dual control works satisfactorily, and our work and our play is a great deal together.

Amelia Earhart

Jesus was a bachelor. —Don Herold

Intellectuals should never marry; they won't enjoy it, and besides, they should not reproduce themselves.

Herold

Everything in life is fairly simple except one's wife.

Herold

Comic-strip artists do not make good husbands, and God knows they do not make good comic strips.

Herold

Men's wives are usually their husbands' mental inferiors and spiritual superiors; this gives them double instruments of torture.

Herold

Marry one woman and you get six.

Herold

Marriage, like death, is nothing to worry about.

Herold

Marriage is an honorable agreement among men as to their conduct toward women, and it was devised by women.

Herold

Marriage is a mistake of youth—which we should all make.

Herold

Marriage: A woman's hairnet tangled in a man's spectacles on top of the bedroom dresser.

Herold

Most wives are nicer than their husbands, but that's nothing; I am nice to everybody from whom I get money.

Herold

If a wife does not cause all your troubles, she at least conveniently symbolizes them at times.

Herold

If it hadn't been for my wife, I couldn't have stood married life.

Herold

Speak up like you do to your wives.

Jimmy Hoffa
administering oaths, 1959

Marriage is a good deal like a circus: there is not as much in it as is represented in the advertising.

Edgar W. Howe

A woman might as well propose; her husband will claim she did.

Howe

His wife is ten years older than he is, and she calls him "Father."

Howe

Before marriage, a girl complains of her kin to her lover, and after marriage he complains of them to her.

Howe

The average girl at eighteen starts out to make a name for herself, but decides at twenty that some man's will do.

Howe

The first mean thing a newly married man does is to notice the pretty girls again.

Howe

At first a woman doesn't want anything but a husband but as soon as she gets one, she wants everything else in the world.

Howe

A honeymoon is a good deal like a man laying off to take an expensive vacation and coming back to a different job.

Howe

To avoid mistakes and regrets, always consult your wife before engaging in a flirtation.

Howe

It's no disgrace for a woman to make a mistake in marrying—every woman does it.

Howe

Every man should have two wives; one to cook for him, and another to amuse him after he has eaten.

Howe

It is a pity that marriage is the only medicine that has so far been discovered to cure a love affair.

Howe

Whoever heard a married man coax his wife to sing?

Howe

No girl who is afraid to stay home alone in the evening should ever get married.

Howe

After a man is married he has the legal right to deceive only one woman.

Howe

When a man goes crazy, his wife is the first to know it and the last to admit it.

Howe

Never tell a secret to a bride or groom; wait until they have been married longer.

Howe

Men have been living a long time, and the most important thing they have learned is that some things should be kept from their wives.

Howe

Nobody works as hard for his money as the man who marries it.

Frank McKinney (Kin) Hubbard

My idea of walking into the jaws of death is marrying some woman who's lost three husbands.

Hubbard

No self-made man ever did such a good job that some woman didn't want to make a few alterations.

Hubbard

A fellow never knows what he would have done till he's been married a couple of years.

Hubbard

Never get married while you're going to college; it's hard to get a start if a prospective employer finds you've already made one mistake.

Hubbard

When you consider what a chance women have to poison their husbands, it's a wonder there isn't more of it done.

Hubbard

A young wife's biscuits make a dandy border for a geranium bed.

Hubbard

Lots of fellows get credit for being self-made when they merely used their wives' judgment.

Hubbard

I heard that a couple from the circus is going to get married next week. They say it probably will be a three-ring ceremony.

Hubbard

The fellow that puts off marrying until he can support a wife isn't very much in love.

Hubbard

A woman would rather marry a poor provider anytime than a poor listener.

Hubbard

Marry in haste and—get a job traveling on the road.

Hubbard

Married life isn't so bad after you get so you can eat the things your wife likes.

Hubbard

Nothing upsets a woman like somebody getting married she didn't even know had a beau.

Hubbard

Marriage is neither heaven nor hell. It is simply purgatory.

Abraham Lincoln

I have now come to the conclusion never again to think of marrying, and for this reason: I can never be satisfied with anyone who would be blockhead enough to have me.

Lincoln
written after a marriage
proposal was refused

Nothing new here except my marrying, which to me is a matter of profound wonder.

Lincoln

Perhaps the saddest lot that can befall mortal man is to be the husband of a lady poet.

George Jean Nathan

A man's wife is his compromise with the illusion of his first sweetheart.

Nathan

I know many married men, and I even know a few happily married men, I don't know one who wouldn't fall down the first open coal hole running after the first pretty girl who gave him a wink.

Nathan

Marriage is based on the theory that when a man discovers a particular brand of beer exactly to his taste he should at once throw up his job and go to work in the brewery.

Nathan

A widow is the financial remains of a love affair.

Nathan

Alimony is a one-man war debt.

Herb Shriner

One of the Crumpacker kids at the age of fifteen went to the courthouse to get a marriage license. When told he was too young, he replied, "Just give me a beginner's permit."

Shriner

All men make mistakes but married men find out about them sooner.

Red Skelton

What makes a marriage last is for a man and a woman to continue to have things to argue about.

Rex Stout

An ideal wife is any woman who has an ideal husband.

Booth Tarkington

Medicine

Before undergoing a surgical operation arrange your temporal affairs. You may live.

Ambrose Bierce

Dentist: A prestidigitator who, putting metal into your mouth, pulls coins out of your pocket.

Bierce

Physician: One upon whom we set our hopes when ill and our dogs when well.

Bierce

Water: A medicine for the cure of thirst.

Bierce

Diagnosis: A physician's forecast of disease by the patient's pulse and purse.

Bierce

Apothecary: The physician's accomplice, undertaker's benefactor and grave worm's provider.

Bierce

Time will never be a great success as a healer as long as we have to pay taxes.

Bierce

Doctors know what you tell them.

Don Herold

Doctors think a lot of patients are cured who have simply quit in disgust.

Herold

If medicine has made so much progress in the last thirty years, how come I felt better thirty years ago?

Alex Karras

The trouble with doctors, I find, is that they seldom admit that anything stumps them.

George Jean Nathan

Our doctor would never really operate unless it was necessary. He was just that way. If he didn't need the money, he wouldn't lay a hand on you.

Herb Shriner

Military

Rear: In American military matters, that exposed part of the army that is nearest to Congress.

Ambrose Bierce

Reveille: A signal to sleeping soldiers to dream of battlefields no more, but get up and have their noses counted.

Bierce

Admiral: That part of a warship which does the talking while the figurehead does the thinking.

Bierce

Riot: A popular entertainment given to the military by innocent bystanders.

Bierce

The man that would rather fight than eat has not survived the last war.

Benjamin Harrison

They [Union soldiers and sailors] gave ungrudgingly; it was not a trade, but an offering.

Harrison

And we must not forget that it is often easier to assemble armies than it is to assemble army revenues.

Harrison

With capability for war on land and on sea unexcelled by any nation in the world, we are smitten by the love of peace.

Harrison

The chains of military despotism once fastened upon a nation, ages might pass away before they could be shaken off.

William Henry Harrison

I haven't seen a draft questionnaire yet in which the guy said he shot people for a living.
—Lewis B. Hershey

It's nonsense to cry that you can't plan your life because of the draft. You can volunteer any time you want to.

Hershey

tell my friends—and I have a great many of them who are conscientious
objectors—that they are a luxury, and if we ever get in a lifeboat where everybody
has to pull an oar, they will have to pull an oar or we will have to throw them
overboard.

Hershey

A good general is never taken by surprise.

Little Turtle

Remember, God provides the best camouflage several hours out of every twenty-four.

David M. Shoup
on night fighting

Money

Draw your salary before spending it.

George Ade

Money: A blessing that is of no advantage to us excepting when we part with it.

Ambrose Bierce

A penny saved is a penny to squander.

Bierce

I'd rather help raise money for museums than for diseases.

Bill Blass

Capitalism without bankruptcy is like Christianity without hell.

Frank Borman

We have been cursed with the reign of gold long enough. Money constitutes no
proper basis of civilization. The time has come to regenerate society.

Eugene V. Debs

I wish I were either rich enough or poor enough to do a lot of things that are
impossible in my present comfortable circumstances.

Don Herold

At its present cost, life is worth about thirty cents on the dollar.

Herold

No man's credit is as good as his money.

Edgar W. Howe

One of the difficult tasks in this world is to convince a woman that even a bargain costs money.

Howe

When a man says money can do everything, that settles it; he hasn't any.

Howe

There is only one thing for a man to do who is married to a woman who enjoys spending money, and that is to enjoy earning it.

Howe

He belongs to so many benevolent societies that he is destitute.

Howe

If a man has money, it is usually a sign too, that he knows how to take care of it; don't imagine his money is easy to get simply because he has plenty of it.

Howe

Money would be more enjoyable if it took people as long to spend it as it does to earn it.

Howe

A man is usually more careful of his money than he is of his principles.

Howe

The world was made for the poor man; every dollar will buy more necessities than it will buy luxuries.

Howe

Only one fellow in ten thousand understands the currency question, and we meet him every day.

Frank McKinney (Kin) Hubbard

When a fellow says, "It isn't the money but the principle of the thing," it's the money.

Hubbard

Money never made a fool of anybody; it only shows them up.

Hubbard

The safest way to double your money is to fold it over once and put it in your pocket.

Hubbard

It makes no difference what it is, a woman will buy anything she thinks a store is losing money on.

Hubbard

No wonder nobody that's got as much money invested in shoes and hose as a woman wants to stick around home.

Hubbard

We may not know when we're well off, but investment salesmen get on to it somehow.

Hubbard

One good thing about inflation is that the fellow who forgets his change nowadays doesn't lose half as much as he used to.

Hubbard

There's too blamed many ways to spend money and not enough new ways to get it.

Hubbard

If a fellow screwed up his face when he asked for credit like he does when he's asked to settle, he wouldn't get it.

Hubbard

It's sweet to be remembered, but it's often cheaper to be forgotten.

Hubbard

A fellow can have more money than brains and still be hard up.

Hubbard

The plainest print cannot be read through a gold eagle.

Abraham Lincoln

The capitalists generally act harmoniously and in concert to fleece the people.

Lincoln

Capital is only the fruit of labor and could never have existed if labor had not first existed.

Lincoln

Other people have trouble to make money, but my trouble is how to dispose of it.

Chauncey Rose

Lots of girls say they want no part of money. After they're married, they still want no part of it—they want all of it.

Herb Shriner

A millionaire is a man with enough lettuce to choose his own tomatoes.

Red Skelton

My doctor said I look like a million dollars—green and wrinkled.

Skelton

Morals

Morality without religion has no roots. It becomes a thing of custom, changeable, transient, and optional.

Henry Ward Beecher

Scenes of passion should not be introduced when not essential to the plot. In general, passion should be so treated that these scenes do not stimulate the lower and baser elements. Sex perversion or any inference to it is forbidden. White slavery shall not be treated. Miscegenation is forbidden. . . . Scenes of actual childbirth, in fact or in silhouette, are never to be represented.

Will H. Hays
Code for the Motion Picture
Producers and Distributors of America Inc.,
1931

Moralizing and morals are two entirely different things and are always found in entirely different people.

Don Herold

A man very careless in his own morals may have the highest ideals for the guidance of the world.

Edgar W. Howe

A thief believes everybody steals.

Howe

None of us can boast about the morality of our ancestors. The records do not show that Adam and Eve were married.

Howe

Changing morals or behavior is no business of mine.

Alfred Kinsey

The moral losses of expediency always far outweigh the temporary gains.

Wendell L. Willkie

Mothers

A mother is the child's classroom.

Henry Ward Beecher

The old-time mother who used to wonder where her boy was now has a grandson who wonders where his mother is.

Frank McKinney (Kin) Hubbard

The hand that rocks the cradle is just as liable to rock the country.

Hubbard

Mothers . . . fill places so great that there isn't an angel in heaven who wouldn't be glad to give a bushel of diamonds to come down here and take their place.

William Ashley (Billy) Sunday

Movies

I wouldn't go on living with you if you were dipped in platinum.

Irene Dunne
in The Awful Truth

Greta Garbo always looks as if somebody had just rescued her from drowning.

Don Herold

Who do you have to screw to get off this picture?

Carole Lombard
of Supernatural

Hollywood is the worst of the dope peddlers because it seeks its opium under a false label. Its customers pull at the pipe in the belief that it is harmless and, when finally they give it up, find that they are still dreaming the former illusions.

George Jean Nathan

Never once got to kiss the girl or be the hero. If I tried to kiss a girl, the hero would come along in the nick of time and kick the heck out of me.

Edward (Tex) Terry

I hate the dawn. The grass always looks as though it's been left out all night.

Clifton Webb
in The Dark Corner

It's lavish, but I call it home.

Webb
in Laura

Murder

Kill: To create a vacancy without nominating a successor.

Ambrose Bierce

Early one June morning in 1872, I murdered my father—an act which made a deep impression on me at the time.

Bierce

Music

A good musical comedy consists largely of disorderly conduct occasionally interrupted by talk.

George Ade

The music teacher came twice each week to bridge the awful gap between Dorothy and Chopin.

Ade

She was a town-and-country soprano of the kind often used for augmenting the grief at a funeral.

Ade

The man who provides the interruptions of a good musical comedy is called the librettist.

Ade

Opera: A play representing life in another world whose inhabitants have no speech but song, no motions but gestures, and no postures but attitudes.

Ambrose Bierce

Phonograph: An irritating toy that restores life to dead noises.

Bierce

The piano is a parlor utensil for subduing the impenitent visitor. It is operated by depressing the keys of the machine and the spirit of the audience.

Bierce

Clarinet: An instrument of torture operated by a person with cotton in his ears. There are two instruments that are worse than a clarinet—two clarinets.

Bierce

While cynics might refer to the little simple melodies [I write] as trash and the words as maudlin sentiment, to me with apologies to none the grandest word in the English or any other language [is] Mother.

Paul Dresser

Oh, the moonlight's fair tonight along the Wabash,
from the fields there comes the breath of new mown hay.
Through the sycamores the candle lights are gleaming,
on the banks of the Wabash, far away.

Dresser

I'd hate this to get out, but I really like opera.

Ford Frick

The chief trouble with jazz is that there is not enough of it; some of it we have to listen to twice.

Don Herold

I would rather sing grand opera than listen to it.

Herold

Don't be ashamed if you can't play the piano. Be proud of it.

Edgar W. Howe

When people hear good music, it makes them homesick for something they never had, and never will have.

Howe

As we grow older we find our admiration increasing for the girl who can't play without the music she has left at home.

Howe

Classical music is the kind that we keep thinking will turn into a tune.

Frank McKinney (Kin) Hubbard

I've put everything into the rock-and-roll business. And I don't think they're going to give me a crown for it in heaven, either.

John Cougar Mellencamp

I care not who writes the laws of a country so long as I may listen to its songs.

George Jean Nathan

My main inspiration for writing a song is a telephone call from a producer.

Cole Porter

In 1940 Artie Shaw made a swing version of it ["Begin the Beguine"] and I've been eating off it ever since.

Porter

George Jean Nathan wouldn't recognize "The Star Spangled Banner" unless he saw everyone else standing up. —Porter

When this horse fell on me, I was too stunned to be conscious of the great pain, but until help came I worked on the lyrics for the song "At Long Last Love."

Porter

My songs have to grow on you.

Porter

I'm a poor little squaw from Indiana,
who embarked on a trip for fun,
I'm a poor little squaw who'll sing "Hosanna,"
when the doggone trip is done.
No, no more shall I roam from my comfy, cozy, Hoosier home.

Porter

Mythic

Mythology: The body of a primitive people's beliefs concerning its origin, early history, heroes, deities, and so forth, as distinguished from the true accounts that it invents later.

Ambrose Bierce

Clairvoyant: A person, commonly a woman, who has the power of seeing that which is invisible to her patron—namely, that he is a blockhead.

Bierce

Mystics always hope that science will some day overtake them.

Booth Tarkington

Nation

Neither the Declaration of Independence nor the Articles of Confederation nor any of the first state constitutions had mentioned the world "republic." At the time it was like a red flag to conservatives everywhere.

Charles A. and Mary Beard

A conservative young man has wound up his life before it was unreeled. We expect old men to be conservative but when a nation's young men are conservative, its funeral bell is already rung.

Henry Ward Beecher

The great nations, like lions roused from their lairs, are roaring and springing upon the prey, and the little nations, like packs of hungry wolves, are standing by, licking their jaws, and waiting for their share of the spoils.

Beecher

It is a noble land that God has given us: a land that can feed and clothe the world; a land whose coastlines would enclose half of the countries of Europe; a land set like a sentinel between the two imperial oceans of the globe.

Albert J. Beveridge

Exile: One who serves his country by residing abroad, yet is not an ambassador.

Ambrose Bierce

Every time Europe looks across the Atlantic to see the American eagle, it observes only the rear end of an ostrich.

Bierce

We want a state of welfare in America and not a welfare state.

George N. Craig

This republic was not established by cowards; and cowards will not preserve it.

Elmer H. Davis

This will remain the land of the free only so long as it is the home of the brave.

Davis

This nation was conceived in liberty and dedicated to the principle—among others—that honest men may honestly disagree; that if they all say what they think, a majority of the people will be able to distinguish truth from error; that in the competition of the marketplace of ideas, the sounder ideas will in the long run win out.

Davis

I have no country to fight for; my country is the earth, and I am a citizen of the world.

Eugene V. Debs

Will it not be wise to allow the friendship between nations to rest upon deep and permanent things? . . . Irritation of the cuticle must not be confounded with heart failure.

Benjamin Harrison

The Yankee intermingles with the Illinoisan, the Hoosier with the Sucker, and the people of the South with them all; and it is this commingling which gives that unity that marks the American nation.

Harrison

Have you not learned that not stocks or bonds or stately homes, or products of mill or field are our country? It is the splendid thought that is in our minds.

Harrison

That which distinguishes us from other nations whose political experience and history have been full of strife and discord is the American home, where one wife sits in single uncrowned glory.

Harrison

It is the great thought of our country that men shall be governed as little as possible, but full liberty shall be given to individual effort, and that the restraints of law shall be reserved for the turbulent and disorderly.

Harrison

In America, a glorious fire has been lighted upon the altar of liberty. . . . Keep it burning, and let the sparks that continually go up from it fall on other altars, and light up in distant lands the fire of freedom.

William Henry Harrison

One thing this country needs is a clearinghouse for coat hangers.

Don Herold

We need some great statements about what America is about and what we can do about it.

Theodore Hesburgh

Just when I get to thinking this is the greatest nation on earth some rotten book comes out and takes it by storm.

Frank McKinney (Kin) Hubbard

Just as in the anatomy of man, every nation must have its hind part.

Robert Indiana

Rome endured as long as there were Romans. America will endure as long as we remain American in spirit and thought.

David Starr Jordan

Fourscore and seven years ago, our fathers brought forth on this continent, a new nation conceived in liberty, and dedicated to the proposition that all men are created equal.

Abraham Lincoln

I recognize the sublime truth announced in the Holy Scriptures and proven by all history that those nations only are blessed whose God is the Lord.

Lincoln

A nation may be said to consist of its territory, its people and its laws. The territory is the only part which is of certain durability.

Lincoln

What this country needs is a really good five-cent cigar.

Thomas R. Marshall

There's only three funny states—Indiana, Texas, and Brooklyn.

Herb Shriner

The trouble with America is bad immigration law.

Asa J. Smith

America is not a country for a dissenter to live in.

William Ashley (Billy) Sunday

I accept the nomination of the Republican Party for President of the United States . . . but I say this, too. In the pursuit of that goal, I shall not lead you down the easy road . . . I shall lead you down the road of sacrifice and service to your country.

Wendell L. Willkie

Our way of living together in America is a strong but delicate fabric. It is made up of many threads. . . . Let us not tear it asunder. For no man knows, once it is destroyed, where or when man will find its protective warmth again.

Willkie

There exists in the world today a gigantic reservoir of goodwill toward us, the American people.

Willkie

Nature

There is everything in a name. A rose by any other name would smell as sweet, but would not cost half as much during the winter months.

George Ade

Flowers: the sweetest things that God ever made and forgot to put a soul into.

Henry Ward Beecher

Flowers have an expression of countenance as much as men or animals. Some seem to smile, some have a sad expression, some are pensive and diffident, others again are plain, honest, and upright.

Beecher

Flowers beckon toward us, but they speak toward heaven and God.

Beecher

You cannot forget if you would those golden kisses all over the cheeks of the meadow, queerly called dandelions.

Beecher

Of all man's works of art, a cathedral is greatest. A vast and majestic tree is greater than that.

Beecher

Of all formal things in the world, a clipped hedge is the most formal; and of all the informal things in the world, a forest tree is the most informal.

Beecher

No town can fail of beauty, though its walks be gutters and its houses hovels, if venerable trees make a magnificent colonnade along its streets.

Beecher

An apple tree in bloom puts to shame all the men and women that have attempted to dress since the world began.

Beecher

October is nature's funeral month. Nature glories in death more than in life. The month of departure is more beautiful than the month of coming—October than May. Every green thing loves to die in bright colors.

Beecher

Cabbage: A familiar kitchen-garden vegetable about as large and wise as a man's head.

Ambrose Bierce

Tree: A tall vegetable. —Bierce

Ocean: A body of water occupying about two-thirds of a world made for man—who has no gills.

Bierce

Air: A nutritious substance supplied by a bountiful Providence for the fattening of the poor.

Bierce

Never have nights been more beautiful than these nights of anxiety. In the sky have been shining in trinity the moon, Venus, and Mars. Nature has been more splendid than man.

Janet Flanner

I am a native Hoosier, and the lakes and streams and hills of Indiana early brought to the boy I used to be courage to carry on through all the years.

Samuel A. Harper

Bees aren't as busy as we think they are. They just can't buzz any slower.

Frank McKinney (Kin) Hubbard

In order to live off a garden, you practically have to live in it.

Hubbard

Any fool can destroy trees. They cannot run away; and if they could, they would still be destroyed—chased and hunted down as long as fun or a dollar could be got out of their dark hides.

John Muir

The clearest way into the universe is through a forest wilderness.

Muir

It is always sunrise somewhere; the dew is never all dried at once; a shower is forever falling; vapor is ever rising. Eternal sunrise, eternal sunset, eternal dawn and gloaming, on sea and continents and islands, each in its turn as the Earth rolls.

Muir

The forests of America, however slighted by man, must have been as great delight to God, because they were the best he ever planted.

Muir

In God's wilderness lies the hope of the world—the great fresh, unblighted, unredeemed wilderness.

Muir

Let children walk with nature, let them see the beautiful blending and communion of death and life, their joyous inseparable unity as taught in woods and meadow . . . and they will learn that death is stingless indeed, and as beautiful as life.

Muir

Climb the mountains and get their good tidings. Nature's peace will flow into you as sunshine flows into trees. The winds will blow their own freshness into you, and the storms their energy, while cares will drop away from you like the leaves of autumn.

Muir

The deeper I delve into natural science the easier it is to see that every created thing has its use . . . and that upon nature keeping her own balance depends the security of the whole.

Gene Stratton-Porter

Noise

Noise: A stench in the ear. . . . The chief product and authenticating sign of civilization.

Ambrose Bierce

A good many people are like automobiles—the cheaper they are the more noise they make.

Frank McKinney (Kin) Hubbard

Nostalgia

Who recalls when folks got along without something if it cost too much.

Frank McKinney (Kin) Hubbard

The sweetest memory is that which involves something which one should not have done; the bitterest, that which involves something which one should not have done, and which one did not do.

George Jean Nathan

Officials

Public men are bees working in a glass hive; and curious spectators enjoy themselves in watching every secret movement, as if it were a study in natural history.

Henry Ward Beecher

Nominee: A modest gentleman shrinking from the distinction of private life and diligently seeking the honorable obscurity of public office.

Ambrose Bierce

Alderman: An ingenious criminal who covers his secret thieving with a pretense of open marauding.

Bierce

King: A male person commonly known in America as a "crowned head," although he never wears a crown and has usually no head to speak of.

Bierce

Anoint: To grease a king or other great functionary already sufficiently slippery.

Bierce

The Senate is a body of elderly men charged with high duties and misdemeanors.

Bierce

If we bar out the irresponsible crank, so far as I can see the president is in no peril, except that he may be killed by the superabundant kindness of the people.

Benjamin Harrison

The president is a good deal like the old camp horse that Dickens described; he is strapped up so he can't fall down.

Harrison

There has never been an hour since I left the White House that I have felt a wish to return to it.

Harrison

The applicants for office are generally respectable and worthy men . . . but at the end of one hundred days of this work the president should not be judged too harshly if he shows a little wear, a little loss of effusiveness, and even a hunted expression in his eyes.

Harrison

Lincoln had faith in time, and time has justified his faith.

Harrison

I am the clerk of the Court of Common Pleas of Hamilton County at your service. . . . Some folks are silly enough to have formed a plan to make a president of the United States out of this clerk and clodhopper.

William Henry Harrison

I have never regarded the office of chief magistrate as conferring upon the incumbent the power of master over the popular will, but as granting him the power to execute the properly expressed will of the people and not resist it.

Harrison

Never with my consent shall an officer of the people, compensated for his services out of their pockets, become the pliant instrument of the executive will.

Harrison

The delicate duty of devising schemes of revenue should be left where the Constitution has placed it—with the immediate representatives of the people.

Harrison

It is absurd to call him [Lincoln] a modest man. No great man was ever modest. . . . I consider Lincoln republicanism incarnate—with all its faults and all its virtues.

John Milton Hay

They all know I'm back, very much back, and that I will be the general president again come hell or high water. I'm not a guy who believes in limited warfare, so the rats better start jumping the ship.

Jimmy Hoffa

After a man has been in Congress, he rarely goes back to real work.

Edgar W. Howe

There are some folks standing behind the president that ought to get around where he can watch them.

Frank McKinney (Kin) Hubbard

The less a statesman amounts to, the more he loves the flag.

Hubbard

The hardest thing to stop is a temporary chairman.

Hubbard

It's pretty hard to underpay a city official.

Hubbard

All the great calamities on land and sea have been traced to inspectors who did not inspect.

Hubbard

Honest statesmanship is the wise employment of individual meanness for the public good.

Abraham Lincoln

As president, I have no eyes but constitutional eyes; I cannot see you.

Lincoln

I have been told I was on the road to hell, but I had no idea it was just a mile down the road with a dome on it.

Lincoln

If I were to try to read, much less answer, all the attacks made on me, this shop might as well be closed for any other business.

Lincoln

Once there were two brothers; one ran away to sea, the other was elected vice president—nothing was ever heard from either of them again.

Thomas R. Marshall

The vice president of the United States is like a man in a cataleptic state; he cannot speak; he cannot move; he suffers no pain; and yet he is perfectly conscious of everything that is going on about him.

Marshall

You know the buck stops here with me. I made the decision, I . . . felt that I had the authority to do it; I thought it was a good idea; I was convinced that the president would, in the end, think it was a good idea, but did not want him to be associated with the decision.

John Poindexter

One word sums up probably the responsibility of any vice president. And that one word is, "to be prepared."

Danforth Quayle

I should have remembered that it was Andrew Jackson who said that, since he got his nickname "Stonewall" by vetoing bills passed by Congress.

Quayle

There are only two powers in the universe that can save you from death. One is God Almighty and the other is Governor James Brown Ray of Indiana. I am Governor Ray and do pardon you.

James Brown Ray

I remember a sheriff we once had. He was honest as the day is long, but of course when it got dark, you had to watch him.

Herb Shriner

Our mail was always slow back home. It wasn't the postmaster's fault . . . he was a slow reader. We didn't mind him reading the mail so much, but we got peeved when he started answering it too.

Shriner

Take the mayor of my home town. He made a campaign speech and said, "Friends, I sure am proud of you citizens in this town and all the things you stand for." And believe me, we stood for plenty.

Shriner

Oil

If there is one symbol of the establishment ripping off the people, it is the oil companies.

Birch Bayh

I am tired of the oil companies determining the price of everything we use that is made from petroleum. I want to break up the monopolistic control they have from the time they punch a hole in the ground to putting gas in the tank.

Bayh

The still groaned and grunted, leaked here and there, and was cantankerous and perverse in many ways.

Robert E. Humphreys

Opinion

There is nothing that makes more cowards and feeble men than public opinion.

Henry Ward Beecher

If public opinion were determined by a throw of the dice, it would in the long run be half the time right.

Ambrose Bierce

One of the commonest ailments of the present day is premature formation of opinion.

Frank McKinney (Kin) Hubbard

Seriously, I do not think I am fit for the presidency.

Abraham Lincoln

It is only the man who has made a thorough study of a subject who hesitates to express an unqualified, absolutely certain opinion.

Thomas R. Marshall

Opportunity

When it is dark enough, you can see the stars.

Charles A. Beard

Opportunity: A favorable occasion for grasping a disappointment.

Ambrose Bierce

I believe also in the American opportunity that puts the starry sky above every boy's head, and sets his foot upon a ladder that he may climb until his strength gives out.

Benjamin Harrison

Opportunity only knocks once and then we're generally in the back part of the house.

Frank McKinney (Kin) Hubbard

Optimism

Optimist: A proponent of the doctrine that black is white.

Ambrose Bierce

Optimism: The doctrine, or belief that everything is beautiful, including what is ugly, everything good, especially the bad, and everything right that is wrong. It is hereditary, but fortunately not contagious.

Bierce

We make most of our mistakes when we are optimistic. —Don Herold

Many of the optimists in the world don't own a hundred dollars, and because of their optimism never will.

Edgar W. Howe

An optimist is always broke.

Frank McKinney (Kin) Hubbard

An optimist is a fellow who believes what's going to be will be postponed.

Hubbard

Being optimistic after you've got everything you want doesn't count.

Hubbard

Let us diligently apply the means, never doubting that a just God in his own time will give us the right result.

Abraham Lincoln

An optimist is a fellow who believes that a housefly is looking for a way to get out.

George Jean Nathan

The reason I like flying kites, you're always looking up.

Ansel Toney

Organizations

The great danger to popular institutions is extravagance.

Walter Q. Gresham

It seems that nothing ever gets to going good till there's a few resignations.

Frank McKinney (Kin) Hubbard

Organs

Hand: A singular instrument worn at the end of a human arm and commonly thrust into somebody's pocket.

Ambrose Bierce

Mouth: In man, the gateway to the soul; in woman, the outlet of the heart.

Bierce

Heart: An automatic, muscular blood-pump. Figuratively, this useful organ is said to be the seat of emotions and sentiments—a very pretty fancy which, however, is nothing but a survival of a once universal belief. It is now known that the sentiments and emotions reside in the stomach.

Bierce

Diaphragm: A muscular partition separating disorders of the chest from disorders of the bowels.

Bierce

Pain

Pain: An uncomfortable frame of mind that may have a physical basis in something that is being done to the body, or may be purely mental, caused by the good fortune of another.

Ambrose Bierce

Patience

Patience: A minor form of despair, disguised as a virtue.

Ambrose Bierce

A woman who has never seen her husband fishing doesn't know what a patient man she has married.

Edgar W. Howe

All things come to him that waits—if he knows where to wait.

Frank McKinney (Kin) Hubbard

A man watches his pear tree day after day, impatient for the ripening of the fruit. Let him attempt to force the process, and he will spoil both fruit and tree. But let him patiently wait, and the ripe fruit at length falls into his lap.

Abraham Lincoln

Patriotism

Patriotism: Combustible rubbish read to the torch of anyone ambitious to illuminate his name.

Ambrose Bierce

Patriotism is as fierce as a fever, pitiless as the grave, blind as a stone and irrational as a headless man.

Bierce

Patriot: One to whom the interests of a part seem superior to those of the whole. The dupe of statesmen and the tool of conquerors.

Bierce

What this country needs—what every country needs occasionally—is a good hard bloody war to revive the vice of patriotism on which its existence as a nation depends.

Bierce

A love of the flag and an understanding of what it stands for should be sedulously promoted in all our educational institutions.

Benjamin Harrison

When a dog barks at the moon, then it is religion; but when he barks at strangers, it is patriotism.

David Starr Jordan

Patriotism is often an arbitrary veneration of real estate above principle.

George Jean Nathan

Peace

Peace: In international affairs, a period of cheating between two periods of fighting.

Ambrose Bierce

Reconciliation: An armed truce for the purpose of digging up the dead.

Bierce

Peace has its victories no less than war, but it doesn't have as many monuments to unveil.

Frank McKinney (Kin) Hubbard

Universal peace sounds ridiculous to the head of an average family.

Hubbard

There are pacifists in pleasure as well as pacifists in war. The latter are called cowards. The former are called leading moral citizens.

George Jean Nathan

When I say that peace must be planned on a world basis, I mean quite literally that it must embrace the earth. . . . It is inescapable that there can be no peace for any part of the world unless the foundations of peace are made secure throughout all parts of the world.

Wendell L. Willkie

People

There are two classes of people: the righteous and the unrighteous. The classifying is done by the righteous.

Ambrose Bierce

People are always neglecting something they can do in trying to do something they can't do.

Edgar W. Howe

I like gentle people, because there are so many in the world who are not gentle.

Ernie Pyle

Philosophy

It is against my trade to blow on my pals. If a man knows anything, he ought to die with it in him.

Sam Bass

The philosophy of one century is the common sense of the next.

Henry Ward Beecher

A cobweb is as good as the mightiest cable when there is no strain upon it.

Beecher

Philosophy: A route of many roads leading from nowhere to nothing.

Ambrose Bierce

Reality: The dream of a mad philosopher.

Bierce

Effect: The second of two phenomena that always occur together in the same order. The first, called a cause, is said to generate the other—which is no more sensible than it would be for one who has never seen a dog except in pursuit of a rabbit to declare the rabbit the cause of the dog.

Bierce

Miracle: An act or event out of the order of nature and accountability, as beating a normal hand of four kings and an ace with four aces and a king.

Bierce

I've got a theory that if you give 100 percent all the time, somehow things will work out in the end.

Larry Bird

Life is a God-damned, stinking, treacherous game and nine hundred and ninety-nine men out of a thousand are bastards.

Theodore Dreiser

The strongest phases of our new American philosophy . . . are the desire for enormous business, more wealth and less liberty, more despotism and less freedom of education, which always accompanies the absolute rule of the few.

Dreiser

Go placidly amid the noise and the haste and remember what peace there may be in silence.

Max Ehrmann

You cannot philosophize your life and live it too.

Don Herold

"The more articulate, the less said," is an old Chinese proverb which I just made up myself.

Herold

Thank God few people live as they believe.

Herold

Women do none of the philosophizing, and have all the philosophy.

Herold

Philosophy is common sense. If it isn't common sense, it isn't philosophy.

Edgar W. Howe

Most philosophers are poor, so most of them give the poor the best of it. —Howe

A philosophy requiring a large volume is too much; a hundred pages are enough.

Howe

You may read and study forever, but you come to no more important truthful conclusions than these two: 1. Take care of your body (eat and exercise properly), and your mind will improve. 2. Work hard, and be polite and fair and your condition in the world will improve. No pills, tablets, lotions, philosophies, will do as much for you as this simple formula. . . . The formula is not of my invention. Every intelligent man of experience since time began has taught it as a natural fact.

Howe

Except for the flood, nothing was ever as bad as reported.

Howe

Devoted to indignation and information.

Howe

If you want immortality, make it.

Joaquin Miller

It is the outstanding mark of the Anglo-Saxon's philosophical provincialism that he places sex on the farcical index expurgatories along with his God, his wife, his dog.

George Jean Nathan

Poetry

My country, 'tis of thee, sweet land of felony, of thee I sing—land where my father fried, young witches and applied, whips to the Quaker's hide, and made him spring.

Ambrose Bierce

Rhyme: Agreeing sounds in the terminals of verse, mostly bad.

Bierce

I don't like to boast, but I have probably skipped more poetry than any other person of my age and weight in this country.

William Jacob Cuppy

In the spring of the year, when the blood is too thick, there's nothing so rare, as a sassafras stick.

James Buchanan Elmore

A poem is no place for an idea.

Edgar W. Howe

Poets are prophets whose prophesying never comes true.

Howe

Nothing makes a poet as mad as a late spring.

Frank McKinney (Kin) Hubbard

I've just been through a terrible experience. I was up all night—having a poem.

James Whitcomb Riley

Politics

Maybe I'll never win anything, but I'm going to keep on trying. The big shots may be able to keep me from winning, but they can't keep me from running.

Edmond J. Aocker

Politician: An eel in the fundamental mud upon which the superstructure of organized society is reared. When he wriggles he mistakes the agitation of his tail for the trembling of the edifice. As compared with the statesman, he suffers the disadvantage of being alive.

Ambrose Bierce

Consul: In American politics, a person who having failed to secure an office from the people is given one by the administration on condition that he leaves the country.

Bierce

Elector: One who enjoys the sacred privilege of voting for the man of another man's choice.

Bierce

Revolution: In politics, an abrupt change in the form of misgovernment.

Bierce

A conservative is a statesman who is enamored of existing evils, as distinguished from the liberal who wishes to replace them with others.

Bierce

Nepotism: Appointing your grandmother to office for the good of the party.

Bierce

Politics is the conduct of public affairs for private advantages.

Bierce

Senator: The fortunate bidder in an auction of votes.

Bierce

Politics: A strife of interests masquerading as a contest of principles. The conduct of public affairs for private advantage.

Bierce

Alliance: In international politics, the union of two thieves, who have their hands so deeply inserted in each other's pocket that they cannot separately plunder a third.

Bierce

Opposition: In politics the party that prevents the government from running amuck by hamstringing it.

Bierce

Presidency: The greased pig in the field game of American politics.

Bierce

Push: One of the two things mainly conducive to success, especially in politics. The other is pull.

Bierce

Representative: In national politics, a member of the lower house in this world, and without discernable hope of promotion to the next.

Bierce

They're playing the shell game with watermelons and wash tubs.

Roger Branigin

A senator who in his eighties is defeated . . . for reelection to a seat he has held for thirty years probably feels even worse about it than he would have felt thirty years earlier.

Elmer H. Davis

I am for socialism because I am for humanity.

Eugene V. Debs

I missed politics like I missed scarlet fever, measles and basic training—not very much.

S. Hugh Dillin

The highways of America are built chiefly of politics, whereas the proper material is crushed rock or concrete.

Carl Graham Fisher

The first words uttered by a Hoosier infant are: "I am not a candidate for any office, but if nominated I will run and if elected I will serve."

Ralph F. Gates

There is nothing so unsatisfactory as political life. The most successful politicians are constantly on the ragged edge of anxiety.

Walter Q. Gresham

Too many so-called respectable men think, or act as if they thought, that it was less disreputable to buy a vote than to sell a vote.

Gresham

I have a great risk of meeting a fool at home, but the candidate who travels cannot escape him.

Benjamin Harrison

Honorable party service will certainly not be esteemed by me a disqualification for public office.

Harrison

When I came into power, I found that the party managers had taken it all to themselves. I could not name my own cabinet. They had sold out every place to pay the election expenses.

Harrison

There is no security for the personal or political rights of any man in a community where any man is deprived of his personal or political rights.

Harrison

When I hear a Democrat boasting himself of the age of his party I feel like reminding him that there are other organized evils in the world, older than the Democratic Party.

Harrison

I said to one of the first delegations that visited me that this was a contest of great principles; that it would be fought out upon the high plains of truth, and not in the swamps of slander and defamation. Those who will encamp their army in the swamp will abandon the victory to the army that is on the heights.

Harrison

The only legitimate right to govern is an express grant of power from the governed.

William Henry Harrison

If parties in a republic are necessary to secure a degree of vigilance to keep the public functionaries within the bounds of law and duty, at that point their usefulness ends.

Harrison

As soon as a man becomes so depraved that he is willing to live by politics, he should be arrested and put in some kind of a reformatory, for such a man is a public enemy; he is willing to make it his business to rob the people by means of unnecessary appropriations, and the creation of unnecessary offices.

Edgar W. Howe

That the politicians are permitted to carry on the same old type of disgraceful campaign from year to year is as insulting to the people as would be a gang of thieves coming back to a town they had robbed, staging a parade, and inviting citizens to fall in and cheer.

Howe

No normally constituted fellow can read a daily newspaper without congratulating himself that he isn't in jail or a candidate for office.

Frank McKinney (Kin) Hubbard

Ever notice how an office seeker's eyesight fails after he gets what he wants?

Hubbard

Some defeated candidates go back to work and others say the fight has just begun.

Hubbard

If there's anything a public servant hates to do it's something for the public.

Hubbard

I wish somebody would make a new Republican speech.

Hubbard

Next to handshaking, nothing has been as overworked and successful as promising to reduce taxes.

Hubbard

We'd all like to vote for the best man, but he's never a candidate. —Hubbard

Politics makes strange postmasters.

Hubbard

Now and then an innocent man is sent to the legislature.

Hubbard

Any Republican will tell you that the tariff on wool makes wool higher and woolen clothes cheaper.

Hubbard

He was a power politically for years, but he has never got prominent enough to have his speeches garbled.

Hubbard

THE INDIANA BOOK OF QUOTES

The lavish and shameful use of money to gain political office wouldn't be so bad if the office ever got anything out of it.

Hubbard

I'm sticking by my president even if he and I have to be taken out of this building and shot.

Earl F. Landgrebe

Don't confuse me with the facts. I've got a closed mind. I will not vote for impeachment.

Landgrebe

Everyone likes to be part of the crowd. But when my convictions said no, I cast the lone vote.

Landgrebe

I have been solicited by many friends to become a candidate for the legislature. My politics are short and sweet, like the old woman's dance.

Abraham Lincoln

A fellow once came to me to ask for an appointment as a minister abroad. Finding he could not get that, he came down to some more modest position. Finally, he asked to be made a tidewaiter. When he saw he could not get that, he asked me for an old pair of trousers. It is sometimes well to be humble.

Lincoln

If ever this free people, if this government itself is ever utterly demoralized, it will come from this incessant human wriggle and struggle for office, which is but a way to live without work.

Lincoln

Politicians are a set of men who have interests aside from the interests of the people and who, to say the most of them, are, taken as a mass, at least one step removed from honest men.

Lincoln

Republicans are for both the man and the dollar, but in case of conflict, the man before the dollar.

Lincoln

To be a politician you must not only be convinced that you are right, but that the man in the other rank is not only a bad American but that if his cause prevails the fabric of democracy will be torn in twain.

Thomas R. Marshall

Long years ago I happened to do something that did not suit a man who had been kind to me in my earlier days. He rebuked me for my course of conduct and notified me that he had made me, and that I was a dirty dog. I could not resist the temptation to respond that if he had made me, I could not well see how he expected me to be anything else than a dirty dog.

Marshall

I am unwilling to put it in the power of any man to dismiss me from a public position.

Oliver P. Morton

Politics is the diversion of trivial men who, when they succeed at it, become more important in the eyes of more trivial men.

George Jean Nathan

You do the policy, I'll do the politics.

Danford Quayle

What the emergence of woman as a political force means is that we are quite ready now to take on responsibility as equals, not protected partners.

Jill Ruckelshaus

He didn't have anything to say, but he mixed it up with the rest of his speech so you wouldn't notice.

Herb Shriner

We had a couple of fellows in politics back home that went down to Washington. We didn't think they were doing nothing. Actually they weren't, but they were so good at it, you couldn't tell.

Shriner

True terror is to wake up one morning and discover that your high school class is running the country.

Kurt Vonnegut

The two real political parties in America are the Winners and the Losers. The people don't want to acknowledge this. They claim membership in two imaginary parties, the Republicans and the Democrats instead.

Vonnegut

A political platform is like a railroad platform—not to stand on but to get in on.
James. E. Watson

The men I knew in the Senate are all dead. But it's the best thing that could have happened to them.

Watson

How can you stand behind a man with Saint Vitus' dance?

Watson
in opposing President Herbert Hoover

I have fought vice all my life and I would never run for an office with vice in it.
Harvey W. Wiley

I enjoyed our talk this morning very much. Frankly I cannot answer your ultimate question [who he would support for office] yet because I have not fully decided.
Wendell L. Willkie

Any man who is not something of a socialist before he is forty has no heart. Any man who is still a socialist after he is forty has no head.

Willkie

Poverty

Poverty is very good in poems but very bad in the house; very good in maxims and sermons but very bad in practical life.

Henry Ward Beecher

Poverty is not a misfortune to the poor only who suffer it; but it is more or less a discomfort to all with whom he deals.

Beecher

Distance: The only thing that the rich are willing for the poor to call theirs and keep.

Ambrose Bierce

Only the very poor can afford to be perfectly frank. Only the man with nothing to lose will dare to speak or write the full truth as he sees it.

Bruce Calvert

Poverty must have many satisfactions, else there would not be so many poor people.

Don Herold

There's another advantage in being poor—the doctor will cure you faster.

Frank McKinney (Kin) Hubbard

It's no disgrace to be poor; but it might as well be.

Hubbard

Power

Make men large and strong, and tyranny will bankrupt itself in making shackles for them.

Henry Ward Beecher

Electricity: The power that causes all natural phenomena not known to be caused by something else.

Ambrose Bierce

Power is insinuating. Few men are satisfied with less power than they are able to procure. . . . No lover is ever satisfied with the first smile of his mistress.

William Henry Harrison

There is nothing more corrupting, nothing more destructive of the noblest and finest feelings of our nature, than the exercise of unlimited power. The man who, in the beginning of such a career, might shudder at the idea of taking away the life of a fellow being, might soon have his conscience so scarred by the repetition of crimes, that the agonies of his murdered victims might become music to his soul, and the drippings of his scaffold afford "blood enough to swim in." History is full of such examples.

Harrison

I consider the veto power . . . to be used only first, to protect the Constitution from violation; secondly, the people from effects of hasty legislation where their will has been probably disregarded or not well understood; and thirdly, to prevent the effects of combinations violative of the rights of minorities.

Harrison

Prejudice

The negro is superior to the white race. If the latter do not forget their pride of race and color, and amalgamate with the purer and richer blood of the blacks, they will die out and wither away in unprolific skininess.

Henry Ward Beecher

A prejudice is a vagrant opinion without visible means of support.

Ambrose Bierce

Hypocrisy: Prejudice with a halo.

Bierce

The prejudices of generations are not like marks upon the blackboard that can be rubbed out with a sponge. These are more like the deep glacial lines that the years have left in the rock, but the water, when the surface is exposed to its quiet, gentle, and perpetual influence, wears even these out, until the surface is smooth and uniform.

Benjamin Harrison

What questions are we to grapple with? What unfinished work remains to be done? It seems to me that the work that is unfinished is to make that constitutional grant of citizenship, the franchise to the colored men of the south, a practical and living reality.

Harrison

I try not to be prejudiced but do not make much headway against it.

Edgar W. Howe

All I ask for the negro is that if you do not like him, let him alone. If God gave him but little, that little let him enjoy.

Abraham Lincoln

The attitude of the white citizens of this country toward the negroes has undeniably had some of the unlovely characteristics of an alien imperialism, a smug racial superiority, a willingness to exploit an unprotected people. . . . When we talk of freedom of opportunity for all nations, the mocking paradoxes in our own society become so clear that they can no longer be ignored.

Wendell L. Willkie

Press

He had been kicked in the head by a mule when young, and believed everything he read in the Sunday papers.

George Ade

Newspapers are the schoolmasters of the common people. That endless book, the newspaper, is our national glory.

Henry Ward Beecher

Nowhere else can one find so miscellaneous, so various, an amount of knowledge contained as in a good newspaper.

Beecher

The ordinary citizen is better posted than the average senator or congressman—the reason is that they read more current literature. In this connection I see only one danger—and it is a grave danger—the purchase by corporations which have "interests to protect," and by enormously wealthy men who have ambitions to serve, of so many newspapers. Newspapers thus owned give the people only such information as will help their owners, suppressing all information that might injure them, on the one hand; and on the other hand, giving them information that will help the owners. This, of course, poisons the source of the people's information, and, so far as their influence goes, makes them a good deal worse than ignorant, because it makes them misinformed.

Albert J. Beveridge

Journalist: A writer who guesses his way to the truth and dispels it with a tempest of words.

Ambrose Bierce

I recognize the etching, but feel you used too much acid.

Roger Branigin
on newspaper criticism

The newspaper is not giving him [the reader] his money's worth if it tells him only what somebody says is the truth, which is known to be false.

Elmer H. Davis

The American press, with a very few exceptions, is a kept press. Kept by the big corporations the way a whore is kept by a rich man.

Theodore Dreiser

For forty years the American press has been lying about me, and now it tries to ignore me.

Dreiser

Golden shackles, by whomsoever or by whatever pretense imposed, are as fatal to it as the iron bonds of despotism. The presses in the necessary employment of the government should never be used "to clear the guilty or to varnish crime."

William Henry Harrison

The liberty of the press is most generally approved when it takes liberties with the other fellow, and leaves us alone.

Edgar W. Howe

News is anything that makes a woman say, "For heaven's sake!"

Howe

The editors of the Chicago Sunday papers seem to know everything.

Frank McKinney (Kin) Hubbard

A newspaper picture makes anybody look guilty.

Hubbard

At home nobody ever bought many papers. You knew what everybody else was doing. You'd just buy a paper once in a while to see if they had got caught at it.

Herb Shriner

Freedom of the press is the staff of life for any vital democracy.

Wendell L. Willkie

Principles

Expedients are for the hour, but principles are for the ages.

Henry Ward Beecher

The bottom principle . . . of our structure of government is the principle of control by the majority. Everything else about our government is appendage, it is ornamentation.

Benjamin Harrison

Next to being wrong, the worst state is to be right and not to know why, or to be right for the wrong reasons.

Theodore Hesburgh

You cannot afford to have things given to you.

Edgar W. Howe

Important principles may and must be flexible.

Abraham Lincoln

If this country cannot be saved without giving up the principle [of the Declaration of Independence], I would rather be assassinated on this spot than surrender it.

Lincoln

The principles of Jefferson are the definitions and axioms of a free society.

Lincoln

Promises

Half the promises people say were never kept, were never made.

Edgar W. Howe

A man will promise women and babies anything to keep them quiet.

Howe

Prosperity

Watch lest prosperity destroy generosity.

Henry Ward Beecher

If prosperity will just return no questions will be asked.

Frank McKinney (Kin) Hubbard

It seems to me that when a fellow has neither the time nor the money to do a thing our celebrated prosperity has reached its limit.

Hubbard

Another bad thing about "prosperity" is that you can't jingle any money without being under suspicion.

Hubbard

Property is the fruit of labor; property is desirable; it is a positive good.

Abraham Lincoln

That some should be rich shows that others may become rich, and hence is just encouragement to industry and enterprise.

Lincoln

Public Opinion

There is nothing that makes more cowards and feeble men than public opinion.

Henry Ward Beecher

Public sentiment is to public officers what water is to the wheel of the mill.

Beecher

Public opinion is the most potent monarch this world knows.

Benjamin Harrison

Public opinion in this country is everything. With public sentiment nothing can fail; without it, nothing can succeed. Consequently, he who molds public opinion goes deeper than he who enacts statutes or pronounces decisions.

Abraham Lincoln

Our government rests in public opinion. Whoever can change public opinion can change the government practically as much.

Lincoln

A universal feeling, whether well or ill founded, cannot be safely disregarded.

Lincoln

Public opinion, though often formed upon a wrong basis, yet generally has a strong underlying sense of justice.

Lincoln

Punishment

Penitent: Undergoing or awaiting punishment.

Ambrose Bierce

Capitalism needs and must have the prison to protect itself from the criminals it has created.

Eugene V. Debs

A whipping never hurts so much as the thought that you are being whipped.

Edgar W. Howe

The greatest punishment is to be despised by your neighbors, the world, and members of your family.

Howe

You are hereby suspended because of a bad memory.

Kenesaw Mountain Landis
to a baseball coach
who could not recall an alleged bribe

Purpose

Plan: To bother about the best method of accomplishing an accidental result.

Ambrose Bierce

The world stands aside to let any man pass who knows where he is going.

David Starr Jordan

With malice towards none; with charity for all; with firmness in the right, as God gives us to see the right—let us strive on to finish the work we are in.

Abraham Lincoln

Men are not flattered by being shown that there has been a difference of purpose between the Almighty and them.

Lincoln

We're all put on earth for a purpose, and mine is to make people laugh.

Red Skelton

Quotes

Quoting: The act of erroneously repeating the words of another.

Ambrose Bierce

The fellow that can quote anything hasn't necessarily got any more sense than a parrot.

Frank McKinney (Kin) Hubbard

Everything I say, you know, goes into print. If I make a mistake it doesn't merely affect me, or you, but the country. I, therefore, ought at least try not to make mistakes.

Abraham Lincoln

Radio

Do you mean to tell me people can actually hear me over this damn dingus?

Samuel (Lew) Shank
giving first radio interview

Relatives

A friend who is very near and dear may in time become as useless as a relative.

George Ade

The richer a relative is, the less he bothers you.

Frank McKinney (Kin) Hubbard

Next to a city the loneliest place in the world when you're broke is among relatives.

Hubbard

Many a family tree needs trimming.

Hubbard

Distant relatives are the best kind, and the further the better.

Hubbard

The hardest thing is to disguise your feelings when you put a lot of relatives on the train for home.

Hubbard

Once in a long time you find enough relatives on speaking terms to hold a family reunion.

Hubbard

Religion

The Bible is God's chart for you to steer by, to keep you from the bottom of the sea, and to show you where the harbor is, and how to reach it without running on rocks or bars.

Henry Ward Beecher

Repentance is another name for aspiration.

Beecher

A Christian is every one whose life and disposition are Christ-like, no matter how heretical the denomination may be to which he belongs.

Beecher

Coming to the Bible through commentaries is much like looking at a landscape through garret windows, over which generations of unmolested spiders have spun their webs.

Beecher

The saddest moment in any preacher's life is when he comes down from his pulpit knowing that he gave the people not the best he knew, but only what they expected.

Beecher

We not only live among men, but there are airy hosts, blessed spectators, sympathetic lookers-on, that see and know and appreciate our thoughts and feelings and acts.

Beecher

The church is not a gallery for the exhibition of eminent Christians but a school for the education of imperfect ones, and a hospital for the healing of those needing diligent care.

Beecher

A Christian is nothing but a sinful man who has put himself to school for Christ for the honest purpose of becoming better.

Beecher

The test of Christian character should be that a man is a joy-bearing agent to the world.

Beecher

The great heresy in the world of religion is a cold heart, not a luminous head.

Beecher

Humanity is God's outer church. Its needs and urgencies are priests and pastors.

Beecher

I pray on the principle that wine knocks the cork out of the bottle. There is an inward fermentation, and there must be a vent.

Beecher

Christians and camels receive their burdens kneeling.

Ambrose Bierce

Pray: To ask that the rules of the universe be annulled in behalf of a single petitioner, confessedly unworthy.

Bierce

Baptism: A sacred rite of such efficacy that he who finds himself in heaven without having undergone it will be unhappy forever.

Bierce

Christian: One who believes that the New Testament is a divinely inspired book admirably suited to the spiritual needs of his neighbor. One who follows the teachings of Christ in so far as they are not inconsistent with a life of sin.

Bierce

Cheerfulness is the religion of the little.

Bierce

Infidel: In New York, one who does not believe in the Christian religion; in Constantinople, one who does.

Bierce

A clergyman is a man who undertakes the management of our spiritual affairs as a method of bettering his temporal ones.

Bierce

Convent: A place of retirement for women who wish for leisure to meditate upon the vice of idleness.

Bierce

A saint is a dead sinner revised and edited.

Bierce

Heaven: A place where the wicked cease from troubling you with talk of their personal affairs, and the good listen with attention while you expound your own.

Bierce

Evangelist: A bearer of good tidings, particularly [in a religious sense] such as assure us of our own salvation and the damnation of our neighbors.

Bierce

Heathen: A benighted creature who has the folly to worship something that he can see and feel.

Bierce

Providential: Unexpectedly and conspicuously beneficial to the person so describing it. —Bierce

Religion: A daughter of hope and fear, explaining to ignorance the nature of the unknowable.

Bierce

Redemption is the fundamental mystery of our holy religion, and who believeth in it shall not perish, but have everlasting life in which to try to understand it.

Bierce

Sabbath: A weekly festival having its origin in the fact that God made the world in six days and was arrested on the seventh.

Bierce

The Methodist Church does not need an educated clergy; an ignorant one is better suited to its membership.

Samuel Bigger

South America must be devilish hard up for preaching.

Levi Brewer
on hearing a Hoosier was named minister to Venezuela

If neither your religion nor your education suffice to keep you healthy and happy, better throw them both overboard and try just plain common sense or take to the Open Road.

Bruce Calvert

We are not driven from behind, but lured from before. Not pushed, but pulled. Magnetized from beyond.

Lloyd C. Douglas

All forms of dogmatic religion should go. The world did without them in the past and can do so again. I cite the great civilizations of China and India.

Theodore Dreiser

If I were personally to define religion I would say that it is a bandage that man has invented to protect a soul made bloody by circumstances.

Dreiser

I don't believe that in order to keep the Creator on good terms with us, we must spend a good part of our time mumbling masses and prayers—Christianity is a life, not a belief, and it follows that we are answerable for the uprightness of our belief and not for its rightness.

Walter Q. Gresham

I would not do for a Methodist preacher for I am a poor horseman. I would not suit the Baptists, for I dislike water. I would fail as an Episcopalian, for I am no ladies' man.

John Milton Hay

By really belonging to nobody except God, you belong to everybody.

Theodore Hesburgh

The lasting works of man are those of the spirit. Without them, monuments are never better than tombs.

Hesburgh

A man can't have his soul and save it too.

Don Herold

Were it not for the fact that Christians have to put on a clean shirt every Sunday morning, we have an idea we would be a very good one.

Edgar W. Howe

Religion is not an intelligence test, but a faith.

Howe

We never doubt a woman's religion after we have seen her at church with old clothes on.

Howe

A religion without a hell is no religion at all.

Howe

Communism and religion are the two trades a fool may succeed at as well as the smartest practical man.

Howe

What we call Protestantism was really a free thought movement; a revolt against religion.

Howe

If you go to church, and like the singing better than the preaching, that's not orthodox.

Howe

I have but to say, the Bible is the best gift God has given to man. All the good Savior gave to the world was communicated through this book. But for it we could not know right from wrong. All things more desirable for man's welfare, here and hereafter, are to be found portrayed in it.

Abraham Lincoln

Friends, I agree with you in Providence; but I believe in the Providence of the most men, the largest purse, and the longest cannon.

Lincoln

I have been driven many times to my knees by the overwhelming conviction that I had nowhere else to go. My own wisdom and that of all about me seemed insufficient for the day.

Lincoln

To be thoroughly religious, one must, I believe, be sorely disappointed. One's faith in God increases as one's faith in the world decreases. The happier the man, the farther he is from God.

George Jean Nathan

When you see a church with a bomb hole in its side and five hundred pretty safe and happy people in its basement and the girls smoking cigarettes inside the sacred walls without anyone yelling at them, then I say the church has found real religion.

Ernie Pyle

Going to church doesn't make you a Christian any more than going to a garage makes you an automobile.

William Ashley (Billy) Sunday

I don't believe your old bastard theory of evolution, . . . I believe it's pure jackass nonsense. . . . If a minister believes and teaches evolution, he is a skunk, a hypocrite, and a liar.

Sunday

Some say revivals don't last. Neither does a bath, but it helps.

Sunday

The church needs fighting men—not those hog-jowled, weasel-eyed, sponge-columned, mushy-fisted, jelly-spined, pussyfooting Charlotte Russe Christians.

Sunday

The world is equally shocked at hearing Christianity criticized and seeing it practiced.

David Elton Trueblood

There is no reason why good cannot triumph as often as evil. The triumph of anything is a matter of organization. If there are such things as angels, I hope they are organized along the lines of the Mafia.

Kurt Vonnegut

People don't come to church for preachments, of course, but to daydream about God.

Vonnegut

Repentance is something more than mere remorse for sins; it comprehends a change of nature befitting heaven.

Lew Wallace

A religious awakening which does not awaken the sleeper to love has roused him in vain.

Jessamyn West

Reputation

The meanest, most contemptible kind of praise is that which first speaks well of a man, and then qualifies it with "but."

Henry Ward Beecher

The best-loved man or maid in the town would perish with anguish could they hear all that their friends say in the course of a day.

John Milton Hay

What people say behind your back is your standing in the community in which you live.

Edgar W. Howe

Atlas had a great reputation, but I'd like to have seen him try to carry a mattress upstairs.

Frank McKinney (Kin) Hubbard

Nothing fades like popularity if it's overexposed.

Hubbard

Die when I may, I want it said of me by those who knew me best that I always plucked a thistle and planted a flower where I thought a flower would grow.

Abraham Lincoln

Revolution

If by the mere force of numbers a majority should deprive a minority of any clearly written constitutional right, it might, in a moral point of view, justify revolution—certainly would if such a right were a vital one.

Abraham Lincoln

The right of peaceable assembly and of petition, and by Article Fifth of the Constitution, the right of amendment, is the constitutional substitute for revolution. Here is our Magna Carta, not wrested by barons from King John, but the free gift of states to the nation they create.

Lincoln

Be not deceived. Revolutions do not go backward.

Lincoln

We must unleash the energies of men, but we must in our revolution save this free way of life, bring well-being to a larger and larger number of people.

Wendell L. Willkie

Reward

Commendation: The tribute that we pay to achievements that resemble, but do not equal, our own.

Ambrose Bierce

Disobedience: The silver lining to the cloud of servitude.

Bierce

Achievement: The death of an endeavor, and the birth of disgust.

Bierce

Riches

I wonder if the founding fathers, when they conceived of the First Amendment, meant to give millionaires the right to buy ads and donate money to put something on TV that is misrepresentation and character assassination. . . . The First Amendment should give us all an equal voice. A millionaire should not get a million-dollar voice.

Birch Bayh

No man can tell whether he is rich or poor by turning to his ledger—It is the heart that makes a man rich—He is rich, according to what he is, not according to what he has.

Henry Ward Beecher

Riches are not an end of life, but an instrument of life.

Beecher

Riches without law are more dangerous than is poverty without law.

Beecher

Very few men acquire wealth in such a manner as to receive pleasure from it. As long as there is the enthusiasm of the chase they enjoy it. But when they begin to look around and think of settling down, they find that that part by which joy enters in, is dead to them. They have spent their lives in heaping up colossal piles of treasure, which stand at the end, like pyramids in the desert, holding only the dust of things.

Beecher

If any man is rich and powerful he comes under the law of God by which the higher branches must take the burnings of the sun, and shade those that are lower; by which the tall trees must protect the weak plants beneath them.

Beecher

A fortune is usually the greatest of misfortunes to children. It takes the muscles out of the limbs, the brain out of the head, and virtue out of the heart.

Beecher

Philanthropist: A rich (and usually bald) old gentleman who has trained himself to grin while his conscience is picking his pocket.

Ambrose Bierce

Finance: The art or science of managing revenues and resources for the best advantage of the manager.

Bierce

Impunity: Wealth.

Bierce

Riches are the savings of many in the hands of one. —Eugene V. Debs

I've sold to every civilized nation, and to some that have not enough civilization to boast of and I'm still not a millionaire.

Richard Jordan Gatling

It must be great to be rich and let the other fellow keep up appearances.

Frank McKinney (Kin) Hubbard

The rich man and his daughter are soon parted.

Hubbard

Gold is good in its place, but living, brave, patriotic men are better than gold.

Abraham Lincoln

Nothing is more admirable than the fortitude with which millionaires tolerate the disadvantages of their wealth.

Rex Stout

Right

A man in the right, with God at his side, is in the majority though he be alone.

Henry Ward Beecher

Stand with anybody that stands right, stand with him while he is right and part with him when he goes wrong.

Abraham Lincoln

Neither let us be slandered from our duty by false accusations against us, nor frightened from it by menaces of destruction to the government, nor of dungeons to ourselves. Let us have faith that right makes might, and in that faith let us to the end dare to do our duty as we understand it.

Lincoln

Rights

I am for the people of the whole nation doing just as they please in all matters which concern the whole nation; for that of each part doing just as they choose in all matters which concern no other part; and for each individual doing just as he chooses in all matters which concern nobody else.

Abraham Lincoln

It is not tolerance that one is entitled to in America. It is the right of every citizen in America to be treated by other citizens as an equal.

Wendell L. Willkie

Romance

Kiss: A word invented by the poets as a rhyme for "bliss."

Ambrose Bierce

A chap ought to save a few of the long evenings he spends with his girl till after they're married.

Frank McKinney (Kin) Hubbard

Sayings

Epigram: A short, sharp saying in prose or verse, frequently characterized by acidity or acerbity and sometimes by wisdom.

Ambrose Bierce

Self-denial

It is not what we take up, but what we give up, that makes us rich.

Henry Ward Beecher

Self-denial is indulgence of a propensity to forego.

Ambrose Bierce

Abstainer: A weak person who yields to the temptation of denying himself a pleasure.

Bierce

Total abstainer: One who abstains from everything but abstention, and especially from inactivity in the affairs of others.

Bierce

Selfishness

Selfishness is that detestable vice that no one will forgive in others and no one is without in himself.

Henry Ward Beecher

Selfishness: Devoid of consideration for the selfishness of others.

Ambrose Bierce

The basis of every human thing is selfishness; we do good as incident.

Edgar W. Howe

I never knew a selfish man who was in the poorhouse or the gutter.

Howe

Sense

If a man can have only one kind of sense, let him have common sense. If he has that and uncommon sense too, he is not far from genius.

Henry Ward Beecher

All are lunatics, but he who can analyze his delusions is called a philosopher.

Ambrose Bierce

One day it occurred to me that I was crazy. So I gave up my job, which was paying me $4,000 a year, took the few dollars I had and went to the woods.

Bruce Calvert

There is nobody so irritating as somebody with less intelligence and more sense than we have.

Don Herold

The average man's judgment is so poor he runs a risk every time he uses it.

Edgar W. Howe

Common sense is compelled to make its way without the enthusiasm of anyone; all admit it grudgingly.

Howe

As soon as a man acquires fairly good sense, it is said he is an old fogy.

Howe

Some folks get credit for having horse sense that haven't ever had enough money to make fools of themselves.

Frank McKinney (Kin) Hubbard

Common sense, in so far as it exists, is all for the bourgeoisie. Nonsense is the privilege of the aristocracy. The worries of the world are for the common people.

George Jean Nathan

I have a sixth sense, not the other five. If I wasn't making money they'd put me away.

Red Skelton

Sex

Oh, what a tangled web we weave when first we practice to conceive.

Don Herold

The only unnatural sex act is that which you cannot perform.

Alfred Kinsey

We are recorders and reporters of the facts—not judges of the behavior we describe.

Kinsey

I don't see much of Alfred any more since he got so interested in sex.

Clara Bracken McMillen (Mrs. Alfred) Kinsey

You know how much I love Pappy [Clark Gable], but to tell you the honest truth, he isn't such a hell of a good lay.

Carole Lombard

Sex touches the heavens only when it simultaneously touches the gutter and the mud.

George Jean Nathan

To the Latin, sex is an hors d'oeuvre; to the Anglo-Saxon it is a barbecue.

Nathan

Sexes

He had heard that one is permitted a certain latitude with widows, and went in for the whole 180 degrees.

George Ade

Here's to man, he can afford anything he can get. Here's to woman, she can afford anything she can get a man to get for her.

Ade

When Eve saw her reflection in a pool, she sought Adam and accused him of infidelity.

Ambrose Bierce

Our vocabulary is defective; we give the same name—virtue—to a woman's lack of temptation and a man's lack of opportunity.

Bierce

Women are not much, but they are the best other sex we have.

Don Herold

A man should be taller, older, heavier, uglier, and hoarser than his wife.

Edgar W. Howe

Men have as exaggerated an idea of their rights as women have of their wrongs.

Howe

No woman ever falls in love with a man unless she has a better opinion of him than he deserves.

Howe

After a woman has looked at a man three or four times, she notices something that should be changed.

Howe

It is this making a hero of a plain plug man, and an angel of an ordinary woman, that is the cause of so much disappointment and divorce.

Howe

It isn't the sissy men who help women most, but the rough, capable ones who can be caught and trained.

Howe

Probably a widower enjoys a second wife as much as a widow enjoys her husband's life insurance.

Howe

When a woman hears a man praising some other woman, she thinks to herself how easily some men are fooled.

Howe

I know what women expect, and give it to them without disagreeable argument—they'll get it anyway.

Howe

Everybody has something: a man has dandruff and a woman has cold feet.

Howe

There never lived a woman who did not wish she were a man. There never lived a man who wished he was a woman.

Howe

Men and women do little else but make trouble for each other, yet if a high wall separated them they would break it down to get through.

Howe

A woman who can't forgive should never have more than a nodding acquaintance with a man. —Howe

The trouble in the world is nearly all due to the fact that one-half the people are men, and the other half, women.

Howe

Some men have no ambition, enterprise, or ability, except about women.

Howe

THE INDIANA BOOK OF QUOTES

Most parents don't worry about a daughter till she fails to show up for breakfast, and then it's too late.

Frank McKinney (Kin) Hubbard

The feller that belittles his wife in company is only trying to pull her down to his own size.

Hubbard

No matter where they are, just one bottle of red pop and some fellows want to hug their girls.

Hubbard

There's nothing smart about winning a girl; shaking one is the real test.

Hubbard

Man thinks he's dealing with an inferior brain when it comes to a woman, and that makes him a sucker.

Carole Lombard

Don't grab a girl the moment you get into a taxicab. At least wait until the driver puts down the flag.

George Jean Nathan

I hold that companionship is a matter of mutual weaknesses. We like that man or woman best who has the same faults we have.

Nathan

The man and woman who can laugh at their love, who can kiss with smiles and embrace with chuckles, will outlast in mutual affection all the throat-lumpy, cow-eyed couples of their acquaintance. Nothing lives on so fresh and evergreen as the love of a funny bone.

Nathan

When people say women can't be trusted because they cycle every month, my response is that men cycle every day, so they should only be allowed to negotiate peace treaties in the evening.

June Machover Reinisch

Sin

When a man sells eleven ounces for twelve, he makes a compact with the devil, and sells himself for the value of an ounce.

Henry Ward Beecher

Compassion will cure more sins than condemnation.

Beecher

Sin is not at all dangerous to society; what does all the mischief is the sinner. Crime has no arms to thrust into the public treasury and the private; no hands with which to cut a throat; no tongue to wreck a reputation withal.

Ambrose Bierce

Being a Baptist doesn't keep you from sinning. But it sure as hell takes the fun out of it.

Roger Branigin

No matter how hard the times get, the wages of sin are always liberal and on the dot.

Frank McKinney (Kin) Hubbard

Nothing so purges the mind of indecency as too much indecency.

George Jean Nathan

Sinners cannot find God for the same reason that criminals cannot find a policeman: They aren't looking.

William Ashley (Billy) Sunday

Size

Minor: Less objectionable.

Ambrose Bierce

More: The comparative degree of too much.

Bierce

Slavery

The autocrat of all the Russias will resign his crown and proclaim his subjects free republicans sooner than will our American masters voluntarily give up their slaves.

Abraham Lincoln

I admit that slavery is at the root of the rebellion, or at least its sine qua non.

Lincoln

If slavery is not wrong, nothing is wrong. I cannot remember when I did not so think and feel.

Lincoln

Let us draw a cordon . . . around the slave states, and that hateful institution, like a reptile poisoning itself, will perish of its own infamy.

Lincoln

In the right to eat the bread . . . which his own hand earns, he [the Negro] is my equal and the equal of Judge [Stephen] Douglas, and the equal of any living man.

Lincoln

Whenever [I] hear any one, arguing for slavery I feel a strong impulse to see it tried on him personally.

Lincoln

I believe this government cannot endure, permanently half slave and half free.

Lincoln

Slavery is founded in the selfishness of man's nature—opposition to it, in his love of justice.

Lincoln

Society

Laws and institutions are constantly tending to gravitate. Like clocks, they must be occasionally cleansed and wound up, and set to true time.

Henry Ward Beecher

If you're going to play in a society such as we're in, you've got to do your share of things that are not fair.

Lewis B. Hershey

The last thing a shaken society needs is more shaking.

Theodore Hesburgh

When we try to pick out anything by itself we find it hitched to everything else in the universe.

John Muir

Sophistication

Sophistication: Knowing enough to keep your feet out of the crack of the theater seat in front of you.

Don Herold

There is more sophistication and less sense in New York than anywhere else on the globe.

Herold

Space

Good-bye, good night, Merry Christmas. God bless all of you, all of you on the good Earth.

Frank Borman

The moon is a different thing to each of us.

Borman

Astronauts are space activists.

Borman

I am not one of those who laugh at the idea of Earth travel by rocket.

Virgil I. "Gus" Grissom

I've been afraid plenty of times. All of us guys [astronauts] will admit it.

Grissom

There have been times when all of us wished we'd gone in for some other line of work . . . but when the first man touches down on the moon a few years from now, well, we'll know that the whole thing has been more than worth it.

Grissom

Mars is essentially in the same orbit. Mars is somewhat the same distance from the sun, which is very important. We have seen pictures where there are canals, we believe, and water. If there is water that means there is oxygen. If oxygen, that means we can breathe.

Danford Quayle

There's a lot of uncharted waters in space.

Quayle

Space is almost infinite. As a matter of fact, we think it is infinite.

Quayle

"One sacred memory from childhood is perhaps the best education," said Fyodor Dostoyevsky. I believe that, and I hope that many earthling children will respond to the first human footprint on the moon as a sacred thing. We need sacred things.

Kurt Vonnegut

Speech

Free speech is to a people what winds are to oceans and malarial regions, which waft away the elements of disease and bring new elements of health. Where free speech is stopped miasma is bred, and death comes fast.

Henry Ward Beecher

All words are pegs to hang ideas on.

Beecher

Lecturer: One with his hand in his pocket, his tongue in your ear, and his faith in your patience.

Ambrose Bierce

Slang is the speech of him who robs the literary garbage cans on their way to the dump.

Bierce

It was because I had a thing to say that nobody else would say, and it was necessary to be said.

Bierce

When you get a reputation and don't charge anything, you get deluged.

Roger Branigin

It is not the brain of the man of today that is working too much—it is his jaws.

Bruce Calvert

I did not know the deceased and so I cannot speak about him, but I do know Purdue University and the work it is doing to prove that alfalfa will be a profitable hay crop, and while we are waiting for the preacher, I shall be happy to make a speech on that subject.

George T. Christie

Conversation is the slowest form of human communication.

Don Herold

Sometimes, when I am called upon to deliver two addresses to the same group, I give my speech backwards the second time. And if I am talking before a gathering of scientists, I frequently start my speech at the center and go both ways at once. Then I'm confused more than ever, and my listeners don't have any idea what I'm talking about. But they usually think I'm profound.

Lewis B. Hershey

Anyone who refuses to speak out off campus does not deserve to be listened to on campus.

Theodore Hesburgh

No matter how much strong black coffee we drink, almost any after-dinner speech will counteract it.

Frank McKinney (Kin) Hubbard

Why don't the fellow who says, "I'm not a speechmaker," let it go at that instead of giving a demonstration?

Hubbard

Nothing sounds as flat as an extemporaneous speech when you read it in the paper.

Hubbard

Of all the substitutes, a substitute speaker is the worst.

Hubbard

The hardest thing about making a speech is knowing what to do with your hands.

Hubbard

No law is stronger than is the public sentiment where it is to be enforced. Free speech and discussion, and immunity from whip and tar and feathers, seem implied by the guarantee to each state of "a republican form of government."

Abraham Lincoln

Words are like glass bullets. They shatter in all directions and some of those bits of glass hurt.

—Red Skelton

People have to talk about something just to keep their voice boxes in working order, so they'll have good voice boxes in case there's ever anything really meaningful to say.

Kurt Vonnegut

Speed

Abrupt: Sudden, without ceremony, like the arrival of a cannon shot and the departure of the soldier whose interests are most affected by it.

Ambrose Bierce

Hurry: The dispatch of bunglers.

Bierce

Inexpedient: Not calculated to advance one's interest.

Bierce

Slow motion gets you there faster.

Hoagy Carmichael

Sports

I was shameless about it. Why, a hundred years from now nobody will remember me for any books . . . but they're going to remember me for that stadium. Yes sir, I wanted my name on there.

George Ade

Basketball is my best friend.

Steve Alford

Monday: In Christian countries, the day after the baseball game.

Ambrose Bierce

I can see why fans don't like to watch pro basketball. I don't either. It's not exciting.

Larry Bird

It's my job to put the ball in the hole and get back on defense.

Bird

I don't like talking about money. All I know is the good Lord must have wanted me to have it.

Bird

There are times you feel like, if you're hitting your shots, that Jesus himself can't even guard you.

Bird

All I know is I had all the fingers I needed.

Mordecai (Three Finger) Brown

All gates I've crashed, I'm here to tell, I'll crash St. Peter and then crash hell.

One-Eyed Connelly
on crashing the
Indianapolis Motor Speedway

The amount of hate mail I get is directly proportionate to the time we beat the point spread.

Lee Corso

Coaching's not a job, it's a privilege.

Corso

I'm thirty-two, but my arm is 110.

Carl Erskine

If a manager of mine ever said someone was indispensable, I'd fire him.

Charles Oscar (Charley) Finley

Prospects are a dime a dozen.

Finley

I always wanted to be a player, but I never had the talent to make the big leagues. So I did the next best thing: I bought a team.

Finley

I've never seen so many damned idiots as the owners in sports.

Finley

Five hundred miles is too long a distance for anyone to drive at high speed. The fellows who try it will be so tired during the last 150 miles they'll be lucky not to crash.

Ray Harroun

I wouldn't drive in another race, not even for twice as much money.

Harroun

The fundamental difference between intercollegiate and professional athletics is that in college the players are supposed to be students first and foremost. This does not mean that they should all be Phi Beta Kappas or physics majors, but neither should they be subnormal students majoring in ping-pong.

Theodore Hesburgh

Shouting on a ball field never helped anyone except when it was one player calling to another to take the catch.

Gilbert Ray (Gil) Hodges

Some men are so mean that when they attend a ball game, they want to see the home team beaten.

Edgar W. Howe

When people go hunting in this vicinity, about all they find to shoot at are signs reading: NO HUNTING ALLOWED ON THESE PREMISES.

Howe

Knowing all about baseball is about as profitable as being a good whittler.

Frank McKinney (Kin) Hubbard

The hardest thing about prizefighting is picking up your teeth with boxing gloves on.

Hubbard

In the company with the first lady ever to qualify at Indianapolis, gentlemen, start your engines.

Anton Hulman Jr.

Gentlemen, start your engines.

Hulman

I want him to go away and say, well, I learned more in basketball than in any class I took at Indiana.

Robert Montgomery (Bobby) Knight

I'll get five guys, whoever they are, like I've always done, to pass, to listen to me, to work hard.

Knight

The ability to prepare to win is as important as the will to win.

Knight

We should send the NBA champs to represent us in basketball at the Olympics. And, if the Russians don't like it, tell them to go to hell.

Knight

You see the bench gives the ass a message, then the ass gives the brain a message.

Knight

Regardless of the verdict of juries, no player that throws a ball game, no player that entertains proposals or promises to throw a game, no player that sits in a conference with a bunch of crooked players and gamblers where the ways and means of throwing games are discussed, and does not promptly tell his club about it, will ever again play professional baseball.

Kenesaw Mountain Landis

Boom, baby.

Bobby Leonard

Do you know what I love most about baseball? The pine tar, the resin, the grass, the dirt—and that's just in the hot dogs.

David Letterman

When everything is said and done, all I will be is the answer to a trivia question.

George McGinnis

Athletic sports, save in the case of young boys, are designed for idiots.

George Jean Nathan

Every successful coach must have a successful quarterback.

Ara Parseghian

A coach has to be a chaplain, a public-relations man, a disciplinarian, a counselor, an educator.

Parseghian

I feel very strongly about the value of passing. I may score forty or fifty points, but I consider it a bad night if I don't have at least ten assists as well.

Oscar Robertson

How can you call that traveling? You never saw that move before.

Robertson

You know boys, just before he died, George Gipp called me over close to him and in phrases that were barely whispers he said, "Sometime, Rock, when the team is up against it, when things are wrong and the breaks are beating the boys, tell them to go in there and win one for the Gipper. I don't know where I'll be then, Rock, but I'll know about it and I'll be happy." Within a few minutes the great Notre Dame gentleman, George Gipp, died. Boys, I'm firmly convinced that this is the game George Gipp would want us to win for him.

Knute Rockne

In the Army game we had but eleven pair of football shoes and when we substituted, the players had to change shoes with each other. —Rockne

Football is not and should not be a game for the strong and stupid. It should be a game for the smart, the swift, the brave and the clever.

Rockne

Never tell them how many lettermen you've got coming back. Tell them how many you've lost.

Rockne

The only qualifications for a lineman are to be big and dumb. To be a back, you only have to be dumb.

Rockne

Prayers work best when players are big.

Rockne

I don't want anybody going out there to die for dear old Notre Dame. Hell, I want you fighting to stay alive.

Rockne

Everybody likes to be a Monday-morning quarterback. It's so easy to call the plays a day or two later.

Rockne

I think I sensed that backfield [the four horsemen] was a product of destiny.

Rockne

If his [George Gipp] untimely end held a touch of tragedy, it was not because of any lack of mental or moral assets on his part, but because nature that had given to him so generously, denied him at the very peak of his career.

Rockne

Football is a game played with the arms, legs, and shoulders but mostly from the neck up.

Rockne

People don't want to see a tug of war . . . they want action and entertainment.

Rockne

Football teaches a boy responsibility—responsibility as a representative of his college, responsibility to his teammates, and responsibility in the control of his passions, fears, hatred, jealousy, and rashness.

Rockne

Although we were not the first to use the forward pass, it can be truthfully said that we were one of the first to learn how it should be used.

Rockne

When I was playing ball I missed twenty years of fishing. After I left baseball I fished twenty years and quit. I was caught up.

Edd Roush

I didn't expect to make it all the way to the big leagues, but I didn't care. I just had to get away from them damn cows.

Roush

In most of my races, I not only struggled for victory, but also for my life and limb.

Marshall W. (Major) Taylor

I felt very certain that no rider, regardless of his size or physique could ever shake me off his rear wheel, and no man ever did.

Taylor

I'm going to try to come back. I might grow ugly, but I'll never grow old.

Tom Thacker

When I was in high school and college, I thought the guys in the NBA always cooled it out until the fourth quarter. It was almost as if they didn't care. Well, it's true.

Isiah Thomas

Gymnastics is 80 percent psychological. You can have a perfect body but go out and blow it because you don't have it on top.

Kurt Thomas

Take me out to the ball game,
Take me out with the crowd.
Buy me some peanuts and Cracker Jack,
I don't care if I never get back.

Albert Von Tilzer

All you have to do to win is keep your foot on the throttle and turn left.

Bill Vukovich

I played in the big leagues thirteen years and the only thing anybody seems to remember is that I made a triple play in the World Series. You'd think I was born the day I made that play and died the day after.

Bill Wambsganss

One of the advantages bowling has over golf is that you seldom lose a bowling ball.

Dick Weber

Success is never final. Failure is never fatal. It's courage that counts.

John Wooden

I'm not saying there's no finesse in the pro game, but the college game is mainly finesse, the pro game is mainly brute strength.

Wooden

It's better to go too far with a boy than not far enough.

Wooden

A coach is a teacher, and like any good teacher, I'm trying to build men.

Wooden

Run fast but don't hurry.

Wooden

If you're not on a great team, you don't get a chance to star.

Wooden

Every golfer has a little monster in him. It's just that type of sport.

Fuzzy Zoeller

Stupidity

Idiot: A member of a large and powerful tribe whose influence in human affairs has always been dominant and controlling.

Ambrose Bierce

Everything he knows he holds in the hollow of his head.

Roger Branigin

It's all right to be closed mouthed and coolheaded if you can be that way without looking stupid.

Frank McKinney (Kin) Hubbard

Some fellows get credit for being conservative when they are only stupid.

Hubbard

Of all the unbearable nuisances, the ignoramus that has traveled is the worst.

Hubbard

Success

It is not the going out of port, but the coming in, that determines the success of a voyage.

Henry Ward Beecher

Success is full of promise till men get it; and then it is a last year's nest from which the birds have flown.

Beecher

Men's best successes come after their disappointments.

Beecher

Success: The one unpardonable sin against one's fellows.

Ambrose Bierce

Sweat plus sacrifice equals success.

Charles Oscar (Charley) Finley

When a man succeeds, he does it in spite of everybody, and not with the assistance of everybody.

Edgar W. Howe

A successful man cannot realize how hard an unsuccessful man finds life.

Howe

Every successful man I have heard of has done the best he could with conditions as he found them and not waited until next year for better.

Howe

If you succeed in life, you must do it in spite of the efforts of others to pull you down. There is nothing in the idea that people are willing to help those who help themselves. People are willing to help a man who can't help himself, but as soon as a man is able to help himself, and does it, they join in making his life as uncomfortable as possible.

Howe

After a fellow gets famous it doesn't take long for someone to bob up that used to sit by him at school.

Frank McKinney (Kin) Hubbard

If at first you do succeed, don't take any more chances.

Hubbard

Success may go to one's head, but the stomach is where it gets in its worst work.

Hubbard

With my own ability, I cannot succeed without the sustenance of Divine Providence, and of the great free, happy, and intelligent people. Without these I cannot hope to succeed; with them, I cannot fail.

Abraham Lincoln

Always bear in mind that your own resolution to success is more important than any other thing.

Lincoln

Let no feeling of discouragement prey upon you, and in the end you are sure to succeed.

Lincoln

If we do not succeed, then we run the risk of failure.

Danford Quayle

The trouble in American life today, in business as well as in sports, is that too many people are afraid of competition. The result is that in some circles people have come to sneer at success if it costs hard work and training and sacrifice.

Knute Rockne

Success is peace of mind, which is a direct result of knowing you did your best to become the best that you are capable of becoming.

John Wooden

Surprise

The hardest tumble a man can make is to fall over his own bluff.

Ambrose Bierce

The worst jolt most of us ever get is when we fall back on our own resources.

Frank McKinney (Kin) Hubbard

Sympathy

Comfort: A state of mind produced by contemplation of a neighbor's uneasiness.

Ambrose Bierce

Condole: To show that bereavement is smaller even than sympathy.

Bierce

Consolation: The knowledge that a better man is more unfortunate than yourself.

Bierce

A sympathizer is a fellow that's for you as long as it doesn't cost anything.

Frank McKinney (Kin) Hubbard

Talk

None love to speak so much, when the mood of speaking comes, as they who are naturally taciturn.

Henry Ward Beecher

When we talk about ourselves we almost invariably use Latin words and when we talk about our neighbors we use Saxon words.

Beecher

Conversation: A fair for the display of the minor mental commodities, each exhibitor being too intent upon the arrangement of his own wares to observe those of his neighbor.

Ambrose Bierce

Least said is soon disavowed.

Bierce

Talk: To commit an indiscretion without temptation, from an impulse without purpose.

Bierce

Loquacity: A disorder that renders the sufferer unable to curb his tongue when you wish to talk.

Bierce

Eloquence: The gift of making any color appear white.

Bierce

Oratory: A tyranny tempered by stenography.

Bierce

Repartee: Prudent insult . . . practiced by gentlemen with a constitutional aversion to violence, but a strong disposition to offend.

Bierce

When a fellow says, "Well, to make a long story short," it's too late.

Don Herold

Many people would be more truthful were it not for their uncontrollable desire to talk.

Edgar W. Howe

There is too much say it, and too little prove it, in the world.

Howe

The fellow that gets ahead of his story wouldn't be so bad if he stayed ahead.

Frank McKinney (Kin) Hubbard

Nobody can talk as interesting as the feller that's not hampered by facts or information.

Hubbard

Very often the quiet fellow has said all he knows.

Hubbard

A good listener is usually thinking about something else.

Hubbard

It isn't a bad plan to keep still occasionally, even when you know what you're talking about.

Hubbard

Television

We're not mining diamonds here. It's rip and read, pure TV.

David Letterman

It doesn't help . . . when prime-time TV has a character . . . bearing a child alone . . . just another lifestyle choice.

Danford Quayle

Television gets worse every year and they're ten years ahead of schedule.

Red Skelton

Life in our country has become one big TV serial.

Kurt Vonnegut

Temperament

Mad: Affected with a high degree of intellectual independence; not conforming to standards of thought, speech and action derived from the conformants from study of themselves; at odds with the majority; in short, unusual. It is noteworthy that persons are pronounced mad by officials destitute of evidence that (they) themselves are sane.

Ambrose Bierce

If you have lived with a cornet player, you can stand anything.

Don Herold

Indignation does no good unless it is backed with a club of sufficient size to awe the opposition.

Edgar W. Howe

I believe in grumbling; it is the politest form of fighting known.

Howe

Every man feels the need of a good woman to grumble to.

Howe

A fellow who refused to neglect his business and follow the crowd is called a grouch.

Frank McKinney (Kin) Hubbard

The chronic grumbler is a church social compared to the fellow that agrees with everything you say.

Hubbard

Some people are so sensitive that they feel snubbed if an epidemic overlooks them.

Hubbard

A grouch escapes so many little annoyances that it almost pays to be one.

Hubbard

Sometimes I regret it when the chair's halfway across the floor.

Robert Montgomery (Bobby) Knight

Temptation

All men are tempted. There is no man that lives that can't be broken down, provided it is the right temptation, put in the right spot.

Henry Ward Beecher

Mountains of gold would not seduce some men, yet flattery would break them down.

Beecher

Why resist temptation; there will always be more.

Don Herold

You must put the worm on the hook before the fish will bite.

James Warren (Jim) Jones

Tenets

An entirely satisfactory man is one who gives his heart to God, his money to his wife, and asks nothing for himself.

Edgar W. Howe

As they say out West, if a man can't skin he must hold a leg while somebody else does.

Abraham Lincoln

I believe in vested rights but not vested wrongs.

Thomas R. Marshall

Theories

A theory is no more like a fact than a photograph is like a person.

Edgar W. Howe

A young man is a theory, an old man is a fact.

Howe

If a disinfectant smells good, it isn't a good disinfectant.

Howe

I have no reason for doing so, but I do believe that human success or human failure is about 10 percent heredity and 90 percent environment; but I have also another theory, and that is that what the world knows as a bad environment may act as a stimulus to a man for bettering his condition.

Thomas R. Marshall

Thought

Meditation is largely a running of the mind mill and it does not do any good to run the mill when there is no grist in it.

Henry Ward Beecher

I think I think; therefore I think I am.

Ambrose Bierce

Decide: To succumb to the preponderance of one set of influences over another set.

Bierce

Reason: To weigh probabilities in the scales of desire.

Bierce

Deliberation: The act of examining one's bread to determine which side it is buttered on.

Bierce

Imagination: A warehouse of facts, with poet and liar in joint ownership.

Bierce

Aristotle was famous for knowing everything. He taught that the brain exists merely to cool the blood and is not involved in the process of thinking. This is true only of certain persons.

William Jacob Cuppy

Nobody has ever thought out anything in a shower bath because it's too fast and too efficient.

Don Herold

We need less action and more acute observation as we go. Slow down the muscles and stir up the mind. —Herold

A new thought is dangerous until people have had a chance to pick at it a hundred years.

Edgar W. Howe

Folks that blurt out just what they think wouldn't be so bad if they thought.

Frank McKinney (Kin) Hubbard

When I'm getting ready to reason with a man, I spend one-third of my time thinking about myself and what I am going to say—and two-thirds thinking about him and what he is going to say.

Abraham Lincoln

The power of imagination makes us infinite.

John Muir

Most men, when they think they are thinking, are merely rearranging their prejudices.

Knute Rockne

Thinking doesn't seem to help very much. The human brain is too high powered to have many practical uses in this particular universe.

Kurt Vonnegut

Time

Present: That part of eternity dividing the domain of disappointment from the realm of hope.

Ambrose Bierce

Yesterday: The infancy of youth, the youth of manhood, the entire past of age.

Bierce

Year: A period of three hundred and sixty-five disappointments.

Bierce

November: The eleventh twelfth of a weariness.

Bierce

Clock: A machine of great moral value to man, allaying his concern for the future by reminding him what a lot of time remains to him.

Bierce

Dawn: The time when men of reason go to bed.

Bierce

Day: A period of twenty-four hours, mostly misspent.

Bierce

When men are not regretting that life is so short, they are doing something to kill time.

Edgar W. Howe

Towns

I guess I'm still the hick from French Lick.

Larry Bird

I know the Southerners well; I have traded in old Kentucky; I have bought stock there and sold stock there. Whatever a Kentuckian tells you, you can depend on; he's fair and square; his word is as good as his bond. I speak what I know. . . . As for the blue-bellied Yanks, I've had dealing with them, too; and you've got to watch them as well as pray; . . . they'll cheat you any chance they get, and make a chance if they don't see one. I tell you the devil will never get his own until he gets the Yanks, and he will be mightily loath to claim them; he knows they wouldn't be in hell six months before they cheat him out of his kingdom and get up a government of their own.

Ben Farmbrough
urging Boggstown to join the South

Weary and disgusted, I threw down my blankets at the roots of a large tree, made a pillow of my saddle, and was soon oblivious to the wrangling of my fellow commissioners. But it was a short nap. The other commissioners awakened me to say they had agreed that, as the youngest commissioner, I should draw straws with the oldest for the honor of naming the county seat.

Adam M. French
on naming Lebanon

Farmers worry only during the growing season, but town people worry all the time.

Edgar W. Howe

There isn't much to be seen in a little town, but what you hear makes up for it.

Frank McKinney (Kin) Hubbard

A town is a place where even a haircut changes the whole appearance of the community.

Hubbard

A small town is a place where a person with a private-line phone is considered antisocial.

Herb Shriner

My hometown had one big trouble. Not enough get-up-and-go. Actually, we'd get up, but there wasn't any place to go.

Shriner

We had a hotel in town. It wasn't much, but at least it had a bridal suite. That was the room with a lock on the door.

Shriner

The town was full of live wires—trouble was, they weren't hooked up to anything.

Shriner

Traits

For parlor use, the vague generality is a lifesaver.

George Ade

He had a way of turning things over with his fork, as if to say, "Well, I don't know about this."

Ade

It takes a man to make a devil; and the fittest man for such a purpose is a snarling, waspish, red-hot fiery creditor.

Henry Ward Beecher

Curiosity: An objectionable quality of the female mind. The desire to know whether or not a woman is cursed with curiosity is one of the most active and insatiable passions of the masculine soul.

Ambrose Bierce

Meekness: Uncommon patience in planning a revenge that is worthwhile.

Bierce

Cunning: The faculty that distinguishes a weak animal or person from a strong one.

Bierce

Eccentricity: A method of distinction so cheap that fools employ it to accentuate their incapacity.

Bierce

Vacillation and inconsistency are as incompatible with successful diplomacy as they are with the national dignity.

Benjamin Harrison

It takes a lot of time to be sentimental.

Don Herold

A man who attends to his morning mail in the morning is letting other people decide how he is to spend his day.

Herold

The way to be nothing is to do nothing.

Edgar W. Howe

I don't know anything as willing and that seems to enjoy its work as a revolving door.

Frank McKinney (Kin) Hubbard

Toughness is in the soul and spirit, not in muscles and an immature mind.

Alex Karras

I'm a slow walker, but I never walk back.

Abraham Lincoln

When a jackass brays, no one pays any attention to him, not even other jackasses. But when a lion brays like a jackass, then the lions in the neighborhood may be pardoned for exhibiting a little surprise.

George Jean Nathan

Travel

The time to enjoy a European trip is about three weeks after unpacking.

George Ade

Railroad: The chief of many mechanical devices enabling us to get away from where we are to where we are no better off.

Ambrose Bierce

Los Angeles stinks and I can say that because I'm not running for anything.

Bill Blass

When you take a baby to church or on the train, be sure to have plenty of cookies and chloroform.

Don Herold

Methods of locomotion have improved greatly in recent years, but places to go remain about the same.

Herold

Americans travel to improve their bragging.

Herold

Guides have annoyed me so, that today I killed one and am having him stuffed for our trophy room.

Herold

I get everywhere early because I am always anxious to get away from the place previous.

Herold

Florida's all right if you can keep from catching a sailfish and going to the expense of having it mounted.

Frank McKinney (Kin) Hubbard

If some people didn't tell you, you'd never know they'd been away on a vacation.

Hubbard

Unanticipated invitations to travel are dancing lessons from God.

Kurt Vonnegut

Almost all travel is lost on teenagers. . . . The young do not discover the world. They discover themselves, and travel only interrupts their trips to the interior.

Jessamyn West

Trouble

The worst feeling in the world is the homesickness that comes over a man occasionally when he is at home.

Edgar W. Howe

The trouble with walking in a parade is that life seems so dull and colorless afterward.

Frank McKinney (Kin) Hubbard

Trust

Anxiety in human life is what squeaking and grinding are in machinery that is not oiled. In life, trust is the oil.

Henry Ward Beecher

Never trust an automatic pistol or a D.A.'s deal.

John Dillinger

In the old days all you needed was a handshake. Nowadays you need forty lawyers.

Jimmy Hoffa

When a man has no reason to trust himself, he trusts in luck.

Edgar W. Howe

No men living are more worthy to be trusted than those who toil up from poverty, none less inclined to take or touch aught which they have not honestly earned. Let them beware of surrendering a political power they already possess.

Abraham Lincoln

I trust God, my wife, and myself. People take kindness for weakness and generosity has the form of a sucker.

Red Skelton

Truth

Defeat is a school in which truth always grows stronger.

Henry Ward Beecher

God sends ten thousand truths that come about us like birds seeking inlet; but we are shut up to them, and so they bring us nothing, but sit and sing awhile upon the roof, and then fly away.

Beecher

Whatever is only almost true is quite false, and among the most dangerous of errors, because being so near truth, it is the more likely to lead astray.

Beecher

Truth: An ingenious compound of desirability and appearance.

Ambrose Bierce

Platitude: All that is mortal of a departed truth.

Bierce

The truth has always been dangerous to the rule of the rogue, the exploiter, the robber. So the truth must be ruthlessly suppressed.

Eugene V. Debs

It is quite true that to the victor belongs the spoils, and to the strong the race but at the same time it is sad to think that to the weak and vanquished belong nothing.

Theodore Dreiser

The bud of victory is always in the truth.

Benjamin Harrison

The truth is accessible to you, and you will find it.

Harrison

Express a mean opinion of yourself occasionally; it will show your friends that you know how to tell the truth.

Edgar W. Howe

Nothing is true except a few fundamentals every man has demonstrated for himself.

Howe

We must be truthful and fair in the ordinary affairs of life before we can be truthful and fair in patriotism and religion.

Howe

I believe I never knew any one who was not ashamed of the truth. Did you ever notice that a railroad company numbers its cars from 1,000 instead of from 1?

Howe

If more men accept a doctrine than reject it, and those who accept it are more intelligent than its opponents, it is as near the truth as we can get at present.

Howe

It's almost got so you can't speak the truth without committing an indiscretion.

Frank McKinney (Kin) Hubbard

Truth is generally the best vindication against slander.

Abraham Lincoln

I believe it is an established maxim in morals that he who makes an assertion without knowing whether it is true or false is guilty of falsehood, and the accidental truth of the assertion does not justify or excuse him.

Lincoln

We better know that there is fire when we see much smoke rising than we could know it by one or two witnesses swearing to it. The witnesses may commit perjury, but the smoke cannot.

Lincoln

Let the people know the truth and the country is safe.

Lincoln

The path of sound credence is through the thick forest of skepticism.

George Jean Nathan

The great weakness of experience as a teacher lies in the fact that truth is so alterable.

Meredith Nicholson

Tyranny

All despotism, under whatever name they masquerade, are efforts to freeze history, to stop change, to solidify the human spirit.

Charles A. Beard

Fascism is a dictatorship, and a dictatorship is an authority possessing irresponsible power. . . . Fascism is an effort to freeze the economic crisis arising from the application of great technology—to freeze it by the pressure of military forces sustained openly or tacitly by the middle classes.

Beard

Only those generals who gain successes can set up dictators. What I now ask of you is military success, and I will risk the dictatorship.

Abraham Lincoln

Unhappiness

Unhappiness is in not knowing what we want and killing ourselves to get it.

Don Herold

I try to have no plans that failure of which would greatly annoy me. Half the unhappiness in the world is due to the failure of plans that were never reasonable, and often impossible.

Edgar W. Howe

Unions

The trade union, which originated under the European system, destroys liberty. I do not say a dollar a day is enough to support a workingman, but it is enough to support a man. Not enough to support a man and five children if a man insists on smoking and drinking beer.

Henry Ward Beecher

I am not a labor leader. I don't want you to follow me or anything else. If you are looking for a Moses to lead you out of the wilderness, you will stay right where you are. I would not lead you into this promised land if I could, because if I could lead you in, someone else could lead you out.

Eugene V. Debs

If capital and labor ever do get together it's good night for the rest of us.

Frank McKinney (Kin) Hubbard

I am glad to know that there is a system of labor where the laborer can strike if he wants to! I wish to God that such a system prevailed all over the world.

Abraham Lincoln

Urbanism

Indianapolis is a sort of person—my uncle or somebody.

Booth Tarkington

The city is permanently cruel.

Kurt Vonnegut

Value

One man's poison ivy is another man's spinach.

George Ade

A man's ledger does not tell what he is, or what he is worth. Count what is in man, not what is on him, if you would know what he is worth—whether rich or poor.

Henry Ward Beecher

A bird in the hand is worth what it will bring.

Ambrose Bierce

Adventure is worthwhile in itself.

Amelia Earhart

The most agreeable thing in life is worthy accomplishment.

Edgar W. Howe

One man's enough is another's privation.

Jessamyn West

Nothing is so dear as what you are about to leave.

West

Vanity

She's the kind of person who spends extra money for a stateroom on a Pullman for privacy and then leaves her door open for publicity.

Don Herold

Vices

The most pathetic object is . . . the man who wants to be a degenerate and can't quite make it.

George Ade

There are many people who think that Sunday is a sponge to wipe out all the sins of the week.

Henry Ward Beecher

Of two evils, choose to be the least.

Ambrose Bierce

Pleasure is more trouble than trouble.

Don Herold

The only guy who needs a bodyguard is a liar, a cheat, a guy who betrays friendship.

Jimmy Hoffa

I don't cheat nobody. I don't lie about nobody. I don't frame nobody. I don't talk bad about people. If I do, I tell them. So what the hell's people going to try to kill me for?

Hoffa

There is no inspiration in evil . . . no man ever made a great speech on a mean subject.

Edgar W. Howe

The reason the way of the transgressor is hard is because it's so crowded.

Frank McKinney (Kin) Hubbard

It has been my experience that folks who have no vices have very few virtues.

Abraham Lincoln

There were so many bootleggers here they almost had to wear badges to keep from selling to each other.

Casey Miller
during Prohibition

Vanity is at the bottom of much of the exercise indulged in by men after their youth is gone; the question of health is of second consideration.

George Jean Nathan

Virtues

There never was a person who did anything worth doing who did not receive more than he gave.

Henry Ward Beecher

Meekness is not a contemplative virtue; it is maintaining peace and patience in the midst of pelting provocation.

Beecher

Fidelity: A virtue peculiar to those who are about to be betrayed.

Ambrose Bierce

Perseverance: A lowly virtue whereby mediocrity achieves an inglorious success.

Bierce

Accountability: The mother of caution.

Bierce

And when the harvest from the fields, the cattle from the hills, and the ores of the earth shall have been weighed, counted and valued, we will turn from them all to crown with the highest honor the state that has promoted education, virtue, justice, and patriotism among the people.

Benjamin Harrison

Men are virtuous because women are; women are virtuous from necessity.

Edgar W. Howe

Virtue must be valuable, if men and women of all degrees pretend to have it.

Howe

Wisdom is knowing what to do next, skill is knowing how to do it, and virtue is doing it.
—David Starr Jordan

I admit I was no angel, I had my faults, but I never threw another rider or committed a dishonorable act.

Marshall W. (Major) Taylor

Voting

Vote: The instrument and symbol of a freeman's power to make a fool of himself and a wreck of his country.

Ambrose Bierce

Recount: In American politics, another throw of the dice, accorded to the player against whom they are loaded.

Bierce

Plebiscite: A popular vote to ascertain the will of the sovereign.

Bierce

Incumbent: A person of the liveliest interest to the outcumbents.

Bierce

Applause, mingled with boos and hisses, is about all that the average voter is able or willing to contribute to public life.

Elmer H. Davis

The man who has come to regard the ballot box as a juggler's hat has renounced his allegiance.

Benjamin Harrison

If any intelligent and loyal company of American citizens were required to catalogue the essential human condition of national life, I do not doubt that with absolute unanimity they would begin with "free and honest elections."

Harrison

Voting is a sacred sacrament.

Theodore Hesburgh

I not only believe majority rule is just, I believe it is best. All men know more than a few; all experience is better than new and untried territory.

Edgar W. Howe

The election isn't very far off when a candidate can recognize you across the street.

Frank McKinney (Kin) Hubbard

Wouldn't the way things are going these days make a fine argument in favor of woman suffrage if we didn't already have it?

Hubbard

You can take a voter to the polls but you can't make him think.

Hubbard

The ballot is stronger than the bullet.

Abraham Lincoln

We cannot have free government without elections; and if the rebellion could force us to forego or postpone a national election, it might fairly claim to have already conquered and ruined us.

Lincoln

Bad officials are the ones elected by good citizens who do not vote.

George Jean Nathan

One friend of mine used to come twenty miles to town just to vote. He never seemed to mind the trip, though. Said it was the only money he made all year.

Herb Shriner

War

It is not merely cruelty that leads men to love war, it is excitement.

Henry Ward Beecher

No country is so wild and difficult but man will make it a theater of war.

Ambrose Bierce

War: A by-product of the arts of peace. The most menacing political condition is a period of international amity.

Bierce

Noncombatant: A dead Quaker.

Bierce

Battle: A method of untying with the teeth a political knot that would not yield to the tongue.

Bierce

The right to think is the real difference between us and the enemy; it is likely to give us ultimate victory in the cold war—or in the hot war, if that should break out.

Elmer H. Davis

The working class who fight all the battles, the working class who make the supreme sacrifices, the working class who freely shed their blood and furnish the corpses, have never yet had a voice in either declaring war or making peace. It is the ruling class that invariably does both. They alone declare war and they alone make peace.

Eugene V. Debs

The master class has always declared the wars; the subject class has always fought the battles. The master class has had all to gain and nothing to lose, while the subject class has had nothing to gain and all to lose—especially their lives.

Debs

The purpose of the Allies is exactly the purpose of the Central Powers, and that is the conquest and spoliation of the weaker nations that has always been the purpose of war.

Debs

When Wall Street yells war, you may rest assured every pulpit in the land will yell war.

Debs

Sooner or later every war of trade becomes a war of blood.

Debs

I am opposed to every war but one . . . and that is the worldwide war of social revolution.

Debs

There is so much that must be done in a civilized barbarism like war.

Amelia Earhart

By Jove, no wonder women don't love war nor understand it, nor can operate in it as a rule; it takes a man to suffer what other men have invented. . . . Women have invented nothing in all that, except the men who were born as male babies and grew up to be men big enough to be killed fighting.

Janet Flanner

The Civil War called for a president who had faith in time, for his country as well as himself; who could endure the impatience of others and bide his time.

Benjamin Harrison

It is cheaper to feed the Indians than to fight them.

William Henry Harrison

It has been a splendid little war, begun with the highest motives, carried on with magnificent intelligence and spirit, favored by the fortune which loves the brave.

John Milton Hay
referring to the Spanish-American War

One of the problems we're going to have to solve is to make the armed forces so popular everyone wants to get in.

Lewis B. Hershey

I've lived under situations where any decent man declared war first. And I've lived under situations where you don't declare war. We've been flexible enough to kill people without declaring war.

Hershey

A conquered foe should be watched.

Edgar W. Howe

I sincerely wish war was a pleasanter and easier business than it is, but it does not admit of holidays.

Abraham Lincoln

If you don't want to use the army, I should like to borrow it for a while.

Lincoln
to Gen. George B. McClellan

Military glory—the attractive rainbow that rises in showers of blood.

Lincoln

I had come to despise and be revolted by war out of any logical proportion. I couldn't find the Four Freedoms among the dead men.

Ernie Pyle

War makes strange giant creatures out of us little routine men who inhabit the earth.

Pyle

Young man, you have been trained at the government school and at public expense, and if you don't know how to command who does? To whom are we to look in such times of peril—can't you accept? You have to.

Joseph Reynolds
to Ulysses S. Grant, 1854

Diplomacy has rarely been able to gain at the conference table what cannot be gained or held on the battlefield.

Walter Bedell (Beetle) Smith

The next war will be fought with atom bombs and the one after that with spears.

Harold C. Urey

One of the many effects of war, after all, is that people are discouraged from being characters. —Kurt Vonnegut

The feeling about a soldier is, when all is said and done, he wasn't really going to do very much with his life anyway. The example usually is: "he wasn't going to compose Beethoven's Fifth [Symphony]."

Vonnegut

What war has always been is a puberty ceremony. It's a very rough one, but you went away a boy and came back a man, maybe with an eye missing or whatever but goddamn it you were a man and people had to call you a man thereafter.

Vonnegut

We . . . imagined [the war] was being fought by aging men like ourselves. We had forgotten that wars were fought by babies. When I saw those freshly shaved faces, it was a shock. "My God," I said to myself, "it's the Children's Crusade."

Vonnegut

Generally speaking, nothing of importance can be won in peace that has not already been won in the war itself.

Wendell L. Willkie

Bayonets and guns are feeble as compared with the power of the idea.

Willkie

A war won without purpose is a war won without victory.

Willkie

We won't be at war with Japan within forty-eight hours, forty-eight days or forty-eight years.

Willkie
December 7, 1941

We didn't win any victory in France because of superior training. We accomplished most of the things we did as a result of youth, pep, courage, and the "orders be damned" individuality initiative of our chaps in most cases.

Samuel Woodfill

When you've been hiking through the mud all night with a full army kit on your back you don't care a hoot whether an aerial bomb is a live one or a dud.

Woodfill

Atomic bombs are terrifying, but ideas are worse.

Woodfill

Every man in the AEF (American Expeditionary Force) was just as much a hero as I am. The opportunity just didn't present itself for all of them to display the gallantry that would win decorations.

Woodfill

Warnings

Admonition: Gentle reproof, as with a meat-ax.

Ambrose Bierce

If I had great influence I should exercise it in warning the people that there is something wrong with every big promise.

Edgar W. Howe

If you go slow others will overtake you, if you go fast, you will exhaust your strength and die young.

Howe

A reasonable probability is the only certainty.

Howe

A good catchword can obscure analysis for fifty years.

Wendell L. Willkie

The society of excess profits for some and small returns for others, the society in which a few prey upon the many, the society in which few took advantage and many took great disadvantage, must pass.

Willkie

Weather

Barometer: An ingenious instrument that indicates what kind of weather we are having.

Ambrose Bierce

Winter has always given me a physical sense of suffering.

Theodore Dreiser

Treat spring just as you would a friend you have not learned to trust.

Edgar W. Howe

Don't knock the weather; nine-tenths of the people couldn't start a conversation if it didn't change once in a while.

Frank McKinney (Kin) Hubbard

Winning

Anyone can win, unless there happens to be a second entry.

George Ade

Victories that are cheap are cheap. Those only are worth having that come as the result of hard fighting.

Henry Ward Beecher

A winner is someone who recognizes his God-given talents, works his tail off to develop them into skills, and uses these skills to accomplish his goals.

Larry Bird

You can win and still not succeed, still not achieve what you should. And you can lose without really failing at all.

Robert Montgomery (Bobby) Knight

The minute I stop winning, they'll start to notice my eccentricities. See, if you win, you're eccentric; if you lose, you're crazy.

Knight

Victory has never been a particularly satisfying thing to me. It's really hard for me to say, "Well, we won."

Knight

You have to pay the price—but if you do you can only win.

Frank Leahy

We count on winning. And if we lose, don't beef. And the best way to prevent beefing is—don't lose.

Knute Rockne

Wisdom

The use of the head abridges the labor of the hands.

Henry Ward Beecher

Aphorism: Boned wisdom for weak teeth.

Ambrose Bierce

Platitude: The wisdom of a million fools in the diction of a dullard.

Bierce

In order to have wisdom we must have ignorance. —Theodore Dreiser

Wit

Wit: The salt with which the American humorist spoils his intellectual cookery by leaving it out.

Ambrose Bierce

Witticism: A sharp and clever remark usually quoted and seldom noted; what the Philistine is pleased to call a "joke."

Bierce

Wit that is kindly is not very witty.

Edgar W. Howe

I remember a good story when I hear it, but I never invented anything original. I am only a retail dealer.

Abraham Lincoln

Were it not for my little jokes, I could not bear the burdens of this office.

Lincoln

Women

There is no slave out of heaven like a loving woman and, of all loving women, there is no such slave as a mother.

Henry Ward Beecher

Women and foxes, being weak, are distinguished by superior tact.

Ambrose Bierce

There is positively no betting on the discreet reticence of any woman whose silence you have not secured with a meat-ax.

Bierce

Witch: (1) an ugly and repulsive old woman in a wicked league with the devil. (2) A beautiful and attractive young woman, in wickedness, a league beyond the devil.

Bierce

In order that the list of able women may be memorized for use at meetings, heaven has considerately made it brief.

Bierce

Here's to women. Would that we could fall into their arms without falling into their hands.

Bierce

You are not permitted to kill a woman who has injured you, but nothing forbids you to reflect that she is growing older every minute.

Bierce

Empty wine bottles have a bad opinion of women.

Bierce

To women in general truth has neither value nor interest unless she can make a particular application of it. And we say that women are not practical!

Bierce

A virtuous woman is the most loyal of mortals; she is faithful to that which is neither pleased nor profited by her fidelity.

Bierce

When God makes a beautiful woman, the devil opens a new register.

Bierce

Female: One of the opposing, or unfair, sex.

Bierce

Damsel: A young person of unfair sex addicted to clueless conduct and views that madden to crime.

Bierce

Woman's body is the woman.

Bierce

A woman absent is a woman dead.

Bierce

Belladonna: In Italian a beautiful lady: In English a deadly poison. A striking example of the essential identity of the two tongues.

Bierce

I have always been more interested in women's wrongs.

Roger Branigin

Women's clubs are baloney. There should be more to a woman's club than just planting graves and placing plaques.

Theodore Dreiser

Why must women torment me so?

Dreiser

You walk into a room, see a woman, and something happens. It's chemistry. What are you going to do about it?

Dreiser

Women must try to do things as men have tried. When they fail, their failure must be a challenge to others.

Amelia Earhart

The woman who can create her own job is the woman who will win fame and fortune.

Earhart

There is no sea wave without salt; there is no woman without fault.

John Milton Hay

Women have a wonderful sense of right and wrong but little sense of right and left.

Don Herold

A lot of women are getting alimony who don't earn it.

Herold

Women give us solace, but if it were not for women we should never need solace.

Herold

Gentlemen prefer blondes, but take what they can get.

Herold

So far as is known, no widow ever eloped.

Edgar W. Howe

A bad woman raises hell with a good many men while a good woman raises hell with only one.

Howe

A woman does not spend all her time in buying things; she spends part of it in taking them back.

Howe

A woman never loafs; she shops, entertains, and visits.

Howe

When you say no to a woman, you must follow it with an explanation.

Howe

A younger woman seems to get as much comfort out of a love letter as an older woman finds in a cup of tea.

Howe

The average girl knows but two adjectives, and they are "horrid" and "cute," which she uses on every occasion from describing Shakespeare to the appearance of a corpse.

Howe

There are lots of good women who, when they get to heaven, will watch to see if the Lord goes out nights.

Howe

A woman ought to be pretty to console her for being a woman at all.

Howe

A woman wants men to have a good time in a women's way.

Howe

Some women seem to be able to entertain everybody but their husbands.

Frank McKinney (Kin) Hubbard

I never saw an athletic girl that thought she was strong enough to do indoor work.

Hubbard

Some girls get all there is out of life in one summer.

Hubbard

She treated her hired girl like one of the family—so she quit.

Hubbard

None but the brave can live with the fair.

Hubbard

I don't know of anything better than a woman if you want to spend money where it'll show.

Hubbard

Every time I read where some woman gave a short talk I wonder how she stopped.

Hubbard

Women are just like elephants to me; I like to look at them, but I wouldn't want one.

Hubbard

No matter how low their necks are cut, or how short their skirts get, we'll always have to take chances on their real disposition.

Hubbard

There are two ways to handle a woman, and nobody knows either of them.

Hubbard

The woman that tries to keep up with the procession doesn't see near as much as her husband who stands on the curb.

Hubbard

Why don't women reformers begin on their sisters?

Hubbard

If a girl knew she looked all right, wouldn't it save her a lot of trouble?

Hubbard

Getting talked about is one of the penalties for being pretty, while being above suspicion is about the only compensation for being homely.

Hubbard

I know no more about women today than when I was in high school.

David Letterman

A woman is the only thing I am afraid of that I know will not hurt me.

Abraham Lincoln

Whatever woman may cast her lot with mine, should any ever do so, it is my intention to do all in my power to make her happy and contented; and there is nothing I can imagine that would make me more unhappy than to fail in the effort.

Lincoln

I have never studied the art of paying compliments to women, but I must say that if all that has been said by orators and poets since the creation of the world, if praise of women were applied to the women of America, it would not do them justice. God bless the women of America.

Lincoln

A man reserves his greatest and deepest love not for the woman in whose company he finds himself electrified and enkindled but for that one in whose company he may feel tenderly drowsy.

George Jean Nathan

Whenever a man encounters a woman in a mood he doesn't understand, he wants to know if she is tired.

Nathan

A man admires a woman not for what she says but for what she listens to. —Nathan

Women, as they grow older, rely more and more on cosmetics. Men, as they grow older, rely more and more on a sense of humor.

Nathan

What passes for woman's intuition is often nothing more than man's transparency.

Nathan

An infatuated young man sought counsel at the bazaar of an ancient and prayed the ancient to tell him how he might learn of his fair lady's faults. "Go forth among her women friends," spoke the venerable one, "and praise her in their hearing."

Nathan

Every fallen monument of female reputation I believe had its origin in keeping night company.

John Purdue

It occurred to me when I was thirteen and wearing white gloves and Mary Janes and going to dance school that no one should have to dance backwards all their lives.

Jill Ruckelshaus

Women's rights in essence is really a movement for freedom, a movement for equality, for the dignity of all women, for those who work outside the home and those who dedicate themselves with more altruism than any professor I know to being wives and mothers, cooks and chauffeurs, decorators and child psychologists, and loving human beings.

Ruckelshaus

I shaped my life and career on the single idea that a woman could do anything within reason a man could do and she deserved equal credit, recognition, and pay for comparable accomplishments.

Blanche Stuart Scott

If the exercise of this right [of citizenship] is necessary to the perfect development of man's mind and whole being; if he feels dwarfed, intellectually by being deprived of that right, will not the same argument apply to women?

Mary F. Thomas

She is waiting for me somewhere in the cool shadows of tonight, and I wait for her. She will love me, and I shall make her famous by my pen and glorious by my sword.

Lew Wallace

In my time and neighborhood (and in my soul) there was only one standard by which a woman measured success—did some man want her?

Jessamyn West

Words

I read for three things: first, to know what the world has done during the last twenty-four hours and is about to do today; second, for the knowledge that I specially want in my work; and third, for what will bring my mind into a proper mood.

Henry Ward Beecher

A broken bone can heal, but the wound a word opens can fester forever.

Jessamyn West

Work

[They were] a people so primitive that they did not know how to get money except by working for it.

George Ade

Work is not a curse but drudgery is.

Henry Ward Beecher

Is the working class oppressed? Yes, undoubtedly it is. God has intended the great to be great and the little to be little.

Beecher

When God wanted sponges and oysters, he made them, and put one on a rock, and the other in the mud. When he made man, he did not make him to be a sponge or an oyster; he made him with feet, and hands, and head, and heart, and vital blood, and a place to use them, and said to him, "Go work."

Beecher

In the ordinary business of life, industry can do anything which genius can do, and very many things that it cannot.

Beecher

Any man can work when every stroke of his hand brings down the fruit rattling from the tree to the ground; but to labor in season and out of season, under every discouragement, by the power of truth . . . that requires a heroism which is transcendent.

Beecher

It is not work that kills men, it is worry.

Beecher

Labor: One of the processes by which A acquires the property of B.

Ambrose Bierce

Work: A dangerous disorder affecting high public functionaries who want to go fishing.

Bierce

We could never get our coffee hot when flying out of Cheyenne because of the altitude—and we were too dumb to know why.

Ellen Church

Capitalist wars for capitalist conquest and capitalist plunder must be fought by the capitalists themselves so far as I am concerned. . . . No worker has any business to enlist in capitalist class war or fight a capitalist class battle. It is our duty to enlist in our own war and fight our own battle.

Eugene V. Debs

The rights of one are as sacred as the rights of a million. . . . Every man has the inalienable right to work.

Debs

The workers are the saviors of society, the redeemers of the race.

Debs

Ten thousand times has the labor movement stumbled and fallen and bruised itself, and risen again; been seized by the throat and choked into insensibility; enjoined by courts, assaulted by thugs, charged by the militia, shot down by regulars, traduced by the press, frowned upon by public opinion, deceived by politicians, threatened by priests, repudiated by renegades, preyed upon by grafters, infested by spies, deserted by cowards, betrayed by traitors, bled by leeches, and sold out by leaders, but, notwithstanding all this, and all these, it is today the most vital and potential power this planet has ever known, and its historic mission of emancipating the workers of the world from the thralldom of the ages is as certain of ultimate realization as the setting of the sun.

Debs

The world's workers have always been and still are the world's slaves. They have borne all the burdens of the race and built all the monuments along the tracks of civilization; they have produced all the world's wealth and supported all the world's governments. They have conquered all things but their own freedom. They are still the subject class in every nation on earth and the chief function of every government is to keep them at the mercy of their masters.

Debs

When a man has had to work so hard to get money, why should he impose on himself the further hardship of trying to save it?

Don Herold

Work is the greatest thing in the world, so we should always save some of it for tomorrow.

Herold

Work is a form of nervousness.

Herold

The American labor force is composed of the most uncommon collection of rugged individualists ever assembled for mutual cause. They like to do their own griping and to solve their own problems. They do not want outside help and instinctively resist it. They were never "joiners"—and that includes unions.

Jimmy Hoffa

A really busy person never knows how much he weighs.

Edgar W. Howe

You can't get anything done unless you do it yourself. And usually you can't do it very well.

Howe

No one can help you in holding a good job except Old Man You.

Howe

When I am idle and shiftless, my affairs become confused; when I work, I get results . . . not great results, but enough to encourage me.

Howe

Stew Nugent has decided to go to work till he can find something better.

Frank McKinney (Kin) Hubbard

What's become of the old-time workman that spit on his hands?

Hubbard

Who remembers the good old-fashioned days when the only time you smelled bacon was when you passed a workingman's home?

Hubbard

Who remembers when we used to rest on Sunday instead of Monday?

Hubbard

We all belong to the union when it comes to wanting more money and less work.

Hubbard

A fellow's usefulness frequently ends when he gets an assistant.

Hubbard

Hardly anybody would work for what they're worth.

Hubbard

It's the fellow that works when there's nothing to do that gets to the front.

Hubbard

One mustn't let himself be too much concerned about powers and rights when there is a job to be done.

John N. Hurty

My father taught me to work, but not to love it. I never did like to work, and I don't deny it. I'd rather read, tell stories, crack jokes, talk, laugh—anything but work.

Abraham Lincoln

The lady—bearer of this—says she has two sons who want to work. Set them at it, if possible. Wanting to work is so rare a merit that it should be encouraged.

Lincoln

The strongest bond of human sympathy, outside of the family relation, should be one uniting all working people, of all nations, and tongues, and kindreds.

Lincoln

As labor is the common burden of our race, so the effort of some to shift share of the burden on to the shoulders of others is the great durable curse of the race.

Lincoln

I am glad to see that a system of labor prevails in New England under which laborers can strike when they want to, where they are not obliged to work under all circumstances, and are not tied down and obliged to labor whether you pay them or not. I like the system that lets a man quit when he wants to and wish it might prevail everywhere.

Lincoln

I don't want to work. I don't propose to work. I wouldn't mind being vice president again.

Thomas R. Marshall

I believe about work as I believe about drink; it should be used in moderation.

George Jean Nathan

A life spent in constant labor is a life wasted, save a man be such a fool as to regard a fulsome obituary notice as an ample reward.

Nathan

I've done lots of work at dinner, sitting between two bores. I can feign listening beautifully. I can work anywhere.

Cole Porter

World

It is a very good world for the purposes of which it was built; and that is all anything is good for.

Henry Ward Beecher

With all its shams, drudgery, and broken dreams, it is still a beautiful world.

Max Ehrmann

Whether or not it is clear to you, no doubt the universe is unfolding as it should.

Ehrmann

The world is made up of a great mob, and nothing will influence it so much as the lash.

Edgar W. Howe

As soon as the people fix one shame of the world, another turns up.

Howe

The world isn't getting any worse; we've only got better facilities.

Frank McKinney (Kin) Hubbard

The world gets better every day—then worse again in the evening.

Hubbard

My attitude to the world? I view it as a mess in which the clowns are paid more than they are worth, so I respectfully suggest that when we get going, we get our full share.

George Jean Nathan

This guy used to sell lightning rods until one night he got caught in a storm with a lot of samples.

Herb Shriner

People are too good for this world.

Kurt Vonnegut

Political internationalism without economic internationalism is a house built upon sand. For no nation can reach its fullest development alone.

Wendell L. Willkie

Writing

Posterity: What you write for after being turned down by publishers.

George Ade

My father sent me to an engineering school to prepare me for a literary career.

Ade

My job all my life has been to circulate around and find out what the neighbors are doing and then write about it.

Ade

Plagiarize: To take the thought or style of another writer whom one has never, never read.

Ambrose Bierce

Proofreader: A malefactor who atones for making your writing nonsense by permitting the compositor to make it unintelligible.

Bierce

English: A language so haughty and reserved that few writers succeed in getting on terms of familiarity with it. —Bierce

The author of the best seller of last week is thought by the police of repeating his offense.

Bierce

Circumlocution: A literary trick whereby the writer who has nothing to say breaks it gently to the reader.

Bierce

Envelope: The coffin of a document; the scabbard of a bill; the husk of a remittance; the bed gown of a love letter.

Bierce

I had thought that there could be only two worse writers than Stephen Crane, namely two Stephen Cranes.

Bierce

Printing broke out in the province of Kansu in A.D. 868: the early Chinese simply could not let well enough alone.

William Jacob Cuppy

I seethed to express myself.

Theodore Dreiser

Genius struggles up. Talent often lingers and wears itself out in journalism unheard of.

Dreiser

I went into newspaper work and from that time dates my real contact with life— murders, arson, rape, sodomy, bribery, corruption, trickery, and fake witness in every conceivable form.

Dreiser

Writing is a pleasant disease.

Max Ehrmann

My poetry is all first class . . . my novels hummers. I don't use as many choice words as some writers, but those that have so many choice words don't have any poetry and that's the difference. Look at old Browning or Kipling. You can read their big, fancy words all day and when night comes, and it's time to slop the pigs, you don't know what you've been reading about.

James Buchanan Elmore

I didn't get a publisher because the best I could do was to get 10 percent, and you bet I'm not going to give the children of my phenomenal fancy to the world just for the fun of it.

Elmore

It's easier to be a Bernard Shaw to the British or American public than it is to be a Bernard Shaw to your own family.

Don Herold

A writing man is something of a black sheep, like the village fiddler. Occasionally a fiddler becomes a violinist and is a credit to his family, but as a rule he would have done better had his tendency been toward industry and saving.

Edgar W. Howe

All of us learn to write in the second grade. Most of us go on to greater things.

Robert Montgomery (Bobby) Knight

The most poignantly personal autobiography of a biographer is the biography he has written of another man.

George Jean Nathan

There is no such thing as a dirty theme. There are only dirty writers.

Nathan

I care not who writes the law of a country so long as I may listen to its songs.

Nathan

Mr._____ writes his plays for the ages—the ages between five and twelve.

Nathan

Indiana is a state where not to be an author is to be distinguished.

Meredith Nicholson

I wrote from the worm's-eye point of view.

Ernie Pyle

Writing any kind of fiction is a sort of explosion. When the explosion has taken place, there's no use going around looking at the debris.

Rex Stout

The greatest service any piece of fiction can do any reader is to leave him with a higher ideal of life than he had when he began.

Gene Stratton-Porter

I had no real success until I struck Indiana subjects.

Booth Tarkington

I was for five years, and more, one of the rejected—as continuously and successively, I suppose, as anyone who ever wrote.

Tarkington

This writer was born in a quiet, lovely little city—Indianapolis, Indiana. That small city exists no more than Carthage existed after the Romans had driven plows over the ground where it stood.

Tarkington

Any reviewer who expresses rage and loathing for a novel is preposterous. He or she is like a person who has put on full armor and attacked a hot fudge sundae.

Kurt Vonnegut

The work [of writing fiction] is exceedingly tedious. It is like making wallpaper by hand for the Sistine Chapel.

Vonnegut

God lets you write, he also lets you not write.

Vonnegut

Writers can treat their mental illnesses every day.

Vonnegut

I myself find that I trust my own writing most, and others seem to trust it most, too, when I sound most like a person from Indianapolis, which is what I am.

Vonnegut

When IBM invented the electronic typewriter everybody thought the company was made up of idiots because nobody had complained about the typewriter as it was.

Vonnegut

I believe it was because I had a dream, and I don't just mean a vision or longing or desire to write a novel. I mean I literally had a dream in the form of a novel.

Dan Wakefield

The publication of my first novel was almost enough to ruin my law practice. Whenever I took a case into court for a jury trial, the opposing lawyer knew that all he had to do was to mention my authorship and I was demolished.

Lew Wallace

Any writer knows he has to pay for his compliments. As soon as he has said, Why, thank you, that's very generous of you, the other person clears his throat and dives into his own writing experiences.

Mary Jane Ward

A writer should describe reality with a touch of unreality, an element of distortion, that's the magic of creativeness.

Jessamyn West

Fiction reveals truth that reality obscures.

West

Writing is so difficult that I often feel that writers, having had their hell on earth, will escape punishment hereafter.

West

There is no royal path to good writing; and such paths as exist do not lead through neat critical gardens, various as they are, but through the jungles of self, the world, and of craft.

West

The writer must be willing, above everything else, to take chances, to risk making a fool of himself—or even to risk revealing the fact that he is a fool.

West

People who keep journals have life twice.

West

Faithfulness to the past can be a kind of death above ground. Writing of the past is a resurrection; the past then lives in your words and you are free.

West

Talent is helpful in writing, but guts are absolutely necessary.

West

Youth

Adolescent: One who is well informed about anything he doesn't have to study.

Ambrose Bierce

Adolescence is a stage between infancy and adultery.

Bierce

Enthusiasm: A distemper of youth, curable by small doses of repentance in connection with outward applications of experience.

Bierce

Our moral mentors told us it was an age of unprecedented license and corruption, and that we boys and girls who had just cracked our shells were a brood of vipers from the pit.

Elmer H. Davis

It is said that there is nothing new under the sun. But the young of each generation always think that there is something new under the moon.

Max Ehrmann

When you can't do anything else to a boy, you can make him wash his face.

Edgar W. Howe

Youth is about the only thing worth having, and that is about the only thing youth has.

Howe

Too much youth, in short, is a bore, since youth lacks variety and has little to fall back upon but animal spirits, which are an even greater bore.

George Jean Nathan

Youth is beautiful because it never comes again.

Nathan

There are two barriers that often prevent communication between the young and their elders. The first is middle-age forgetfulness of the fact that they themselves are no longer young. The second is youthful ignorance of the fact that the middle-aged are still alive.

Jessamyn West

If it occurs to a young person, looking at us, that this is the direction in which he himself travels, how can he forgive, let alone bear the sight of us, who constantly bring him the bad news of our own faces, bitter signposts pointing to his own destination?

West

Quotes about Hoosiers

Knute Rockne liked "bad losers." He said "good losers" lose too often.

George Allen

The feet of [Theodore] Dreiser are making a path for us. They are tramping through the wilderness making a path.

Sherwood Anderson

On one of those maple-red Indiana noons, a girl in a rusty Ford smiled at me, for no reason, and without one beat of transition, scruffy kids in knickers went skipping down the alleys of little Hoosier towns, yellow mongrels yapped circles of joy around them: and Model T's chugged past, saying familiar things, like a HOO-ga; and the maple-bright Indiana soon was the color of brick schoolhouses and cherries in Mason jars and firecrackers and sunburn and maple trees gone blazing.

Philip Appleman

Listen kid, take my advice, never hate a song that has sold a half-million copies.

Irving Berlin
to Cole Porter

Her hair looks as if someone ran a brush through it and then said, "Oh, the hell with it."

Mr. [Earl] Blackwell
of Anne Baxter

If he'd [James Dean] lived, they'd have discovered he wasn't a legend.

Humphrey Bogart

I mean to ride into the plaza at Santa Fe, hitch my horse in front of the palace, and put a bullet through Lew Wallace.

William Bonney
Billy the Kid

James Dean epitomized the very thing that's campily respected today; the male hustler. He had quite a sordid little reputation. I admired him immensely.

David Bowie

His features resembled a fossilized washrag.

Alan Brien
of Steve McQueen

I don't like to deal in rumors, but I heard that the guy who took Dan Quayle's law boards for him, *he* cheated.

Albert Brooks

His career typifies the heights to which dramatic talent may carry a man in America if only he has the foresight not to go on the stage.

Heywood Broun
of Kenesaw Mountain Landis

Indiana, a lovely name, musical and lingering upon the tongue. It is a beautiful state, in many ways the most typical of our entire country, or so I feel, when I am traveling through it.

Pearl S. Buck

Welsh, English, Scotch-Irish, and German—these provided the stock that built Indiana into a prosperous community, hearty and tenacious.

Buck

He was one of the most churlish, disagreeable men I ever met in my life; always thinking that everybody was cheating him.

Bennett Cerf
of Theodore Dreiser

He didn't know a baseball from a bale of hay.

Happy Chandler
of Kenesaw Mountain Landis

All living Indianans are active politicians and frequently the dead ones are, too; they've voted them in close elections out there, often.

Irving S. Cobb

Intense, moody, incredible charisma, short, myopic, not good looking. You know who he was like? A young Woody Allen.

Joan Collins
of James Dean

You may fire when ready, Gridley.

Cmdr. George Dewey
to Captain Charles V. Gridley
of Logansport
in the Battle of Manila Bay

When an eastern man is cheated by a Hoosier, he is said to be *Wabashed.*
Ralph Waldo Emerson

Johnnie liked to dance and liked to hunt. . . . I think he liked gravy better than anything else. He liked bread and gravy.

Billie Frechette
about her boyfriend,
John Dillinger

Indianapolis: the largest city in North America with so few natural advantages. It is not on a river of any moment. It is not on a sea. It is not in an area of compelling beauty. It's not warm in winter or cool in summer. It is not near great mineral wealth. In fact, it's not near much of anything. Its detractors refer to it as Indian-no-place, and decry its lack of character.

Joel Garreau

My home is in New York, but my heart is in Gary, Indiana.

Judge Elbert Henry Gary,
who never lived in the
city named in his honor

[I came to] a small town fastened to a field in Indiana. Twice there have been twelve hundred people here to answer to the census. The town is outstandingly neat and shady, and always puts its best side to the highway. On one lawn there's even a wood or plastic iron deer. . . . Down the back streets the asphalt crumbles into gravel. There's Westbook's, with geraniums, Horsefall's, Mott's. The sidewalk shatters. Gravel dust rises like breath behind the wagons. And I am in retirement from love.

William Gass

Charlie Finley wouldn't think God would make a good commissioner.

Warren Giles

The people [in Indiana] are gentle and easy spoken . . . all very sweet and kind Americans. But I can feel an *intolerance* in the air. We are *freer* in the East, and say what we think. In the West, I should be first mobbed with praise and then, if I differed, with rotten eggs. People are *freer from West to East*. In the West they are terrible drinkers—they must be topers or temperance, just as they must be saints or sinners. The people are *freer* only as they are *rude* here.

William Dean Howells

We had a common bond on the A's [Athletics baseball team]: everybody hated Charlie Finley.

Reggie Jackson

I can honestly say he's the most difficult actor I've ever worked with.

Norman Jewison
of Steve McQueen

The bus roared through Indiana cornfields that night; the moon illuminated the ghostly gathered husks.

Jack Kerouac

The Secret Service is under orders that if [President George] Bush is shot, to shoot [Vice President Dan] Quayle.

John Kerry

He was the gangliest, most awkward fellow that ever stepped over a ten-rail snake fence; he had to duck to get through a door; he appeared to be all joints.

Thomas Lincoln
of his son Abraham

When Charlie [Finley] had his heart operation it took eight hours—seven-and-a-half just to find his heart.

Steve McCatty

The president [Abraham Lincoln] is nothing more than a well-meaning baboon. . . . What a specimen to be at the head of our affairs now.

George McClellan

One thing about Steve [McQueen], he didn't like the women in his life to have balls.

Ali MacGraw

An Indiana peasant, snuffling absurdly over imbecile sentimentalities, giving a grave ear to quackeries, snorting and eye rolling with the best of them.

H. L. Mencken
of Theodore Dreiser

Dan Quayle deserves to be vice president like Elvis deserved his black belt in karate.

Dennis Miller

A Steve McQueen performance just naturally lends itself to monotony. Steve doesn't bring much to the party.

Robert Mitchum

Summer in northwest Indiana has been known to produce wistful longings for hell.

Bill Moyers

Richmond, Indiana, where the principles of the American Legion are as deeply rooted as the oil depletion allowance in Texas.

Moyers

[Charlie] Finley is a self-made man who worships his creator.

Jim Murray

Tom's a nice boy—a nice boy—but he just won't get out of that saloon.

Carry Nation
when asked about
Indianapolis
mayor Thomas Taggart

Indiana: No blustering summit or coarse gorge; no flora lurid as disaster flares; no great vacuities where tourists gape nor mountains hoarding their heights like millionaires, more delicate; the ten-foot knolls give flavor of hill to Indiana souls.

John F. Nims

It [southern Indiana] was a wild region, an area of dense forests and grapevine thickets so entangled that travelers often had to cut their way with axes.

Stephen B. Oates

The reading of *Dawn* is a strain upon many parts, but the worse wear and tear fall upon the forearms.

Dorothy Parker
of Theodore Dreiser's novel

If Booth Tarkington were to write *Seventeen* today, he would have to call it *Twelve*.

Arthur Pearl, 1967

One seasoned observer of the Indiana scene suggested to us there was only one place on the globe comparable to Lake County—Hong Kong. "The two places suffer jointly," he said, "from I don't-care-itis, a disease for which no serum has been found. Whether it's vice, prostitution, politics, or crime, everybody in Lake County has a stake in the action or he's a victim of the same."

Neil R. Peirce and John Keefe

What chain of events fostered the narrow provincialism of Indiana? Perhaps it was the state's unfortunate location in the path of America's westward expansion. . . . While access to Indiana is easy, so is access through and out of it: many of its sons and daughters left the state to find their fortunes elsewhere, leaving behind an increasingly inbred, unwavering white, Anglo Saxon Protestant culture with little imagination and equal innovation.

Peirce and Keefe

Indiana, in the first half of this century, had a history of bigotry unequaled north of the Mason-Dixon Line. Indeed, the Ku Klux Klan, hawking its familiar anti-Semitic, anti-Catholic, anti-black propaganda, openly flourished and actually laid legitimate claims to controlling the governor, legislature, and many courts and local government. Yet Indianapolis was the only northern city of its size to escape major racial disturbances in the late 1960s, and remained calm even though embroiled in the trauma of a major school busing court case during the 1970s.

Peirce and Keefe

An empty suit that goes to funerals and plays golf.

Ross Perot
referring to Dan Quayle

Anyone who knows Dan Quayle knows he would rather play golf than have sex any day.

Marilyn Quayle

He [Dan] could pick up his clothes a little more.

Quayle

Bobby Knight is a good friend of mine. But if I ever need a heart transplant, I want his. It's never been used.

George Raveling

God was feeling mighty good when he created Gene Debs, and he didn't have anything else to do all day.

James Whitcomb Riley

Lincoln went down in history as "Honest Abe," but he never was a jockey. If he had been a jockey he might have gone down as just "Abe."

Will Rogers

A cold-blooded, narrow-minded, obstinate, timid old psalm-singing politician.

Theodore Roosevelt
of Benjamin Harrison

For most males in Indiana, a real good time consisted of putting on bib overalls and a cap bearing the name of a farm equipment company and sauntering to a gas station to sit around and gossip about how Elmer couldn't get his pickup truck started that morning.

Mike Royko

Its [Indiana] only large cities are Indianapolis and Gary, which give you the choice of dying of boredom or of multiple gun and stab wounds.

Royko

As for the look on Dan Quayle's face—how to describe it? Well, let's see. If a tree fell in a forest and no one was there to hear it, it might sound like Dan Quayle looks.

Tom Shales

Indiana felt like ice, yet holds wide lakes against that pain: I lived in Indiana once, put these hands into those lakes of counties near Fort Wayne.

William Stafford

Burton wants to blow the whole state of Indiana into Lake Michigan.

Standard Oil board member
when William M. Burton asked
for $1 million to begin
distilling gasoline
using heat and pressure

Judge Gary never saw a blast furnace until after his death.

Benjamin Stolberg
on Elbert H. Gary,
chairman of the board
of United States Steel

Look at John Hay and me. . . . He is secretary of state and I am a gentleman.

Mark Twain

A remarkably handsome man when he is in the full tide of sermonizing, and his face is lit up with animation, but he is as homely as a singed cat when he isn't doing anything.

Mark Twain,
referring to Henry Ward Beecher

Indianapolis, an alien, bustling city oddly out of place in the dreamy Hoosierland of [bucolic poet] James Whitcomb Riley.

Douglas Waitley

Biographies

A

Ade, George (1866–1944): born Kentland; humorist; playwright; author.

Aocker, Edmond J. (1904–1982): Indianapolis resident who changed his name from Rocker to Aocker in 1966 so he would be atop the ballot; ran in primary elections for fifteen various offices.

Appleseed, Johnny (1774–1845): real name John Chapman; born Massachusetts; traveled the Midwest planting apple trees; buried in Fort Wayne.

B

Bass, Sam (1851–1878): born Woodville; became notorious bandit in the West; fatally shot in an ambush after betrayal by one of his gang members.

Baxter, Anne (1923–1985): born Michigan City; Academy Award-winning actress.

Bayh, Birch (1928–): born Terre Haute; state representative; U.S. senator, 1963–81.

Beard, Charles Austin (1874–1948): born Knightstown; historian; educator; writer.

Beard, Mary Ritter (1876–1958): born Indianapolis; doctorate from DePauw University; wife of Charles Austin Beard and collaborator in his historical writings.

Beecher, Henry Ward (1813–1887): born Litchfield, Connecticut; had churches in Lawrenceburg and Indianapolis, 1837–47; lecturer.

Beveridge, Albert J. (1862–1927): born Highland County, Ohio; U.S. senator from Indiana, 1899–1911; foe of Franklin D. Roosevelt; biographer of John Marshall and Abraham Lincoln.

Bierce, Ambrose (1842–1914): born Meigs County, Ohio; grew up in Warsaw from age about six to fifteen; worked in Elkhart; satirist and journalist, mostly with the *San Francisco Examiner*; disappeared in Mexico.

Bigger, Samuel (1802–1846): born Ohio; lawyer at Liberty; Indiana governor, 1840–43.

Bird, Larry (1961–): born West Baden; grew up in French Lick; played basketball at Indiana State University; played with NBA Boston Celtics; coached NBA Indiana Pacers; became president of Pacers' basketball operations in 2003.

Blass, Bill (1922–2002): born Fort Wayne; internationally known clothing designer.

Borman, Frank (1928–): born Gary; astronaut.

Bowen, Otis R. (1918–): born near Rochester; attended Indiana University; Indiana governor, 1973–80; secretary of health and human services, 1985–89.

Bowers, Claude G. (1878–1958): born Westfield; reporter; author; friend of Franklin D. Roosevelt; ambassador to Spain and Chile.

Branigin, Roger (1902–1975): born Franklin; lawyer; Indiana governor, 1965–69.

Brewer, Levi (dates unknown): Madison County resident.

Brown, James Ray (1794–1848): born Kentucky; Indiana governor, 1825–31.

Brown, Mordecai (Three-Finger) (1876–1948): born Nyesville in Parke County; professional baseball player; inducted in Baseball Hall of Fame, 1949.

Butz, Earl L. (1909–): born Albion; researcher, teacher, and dean at Purdue University; secretary of agriculture, 1971–74.

C

Calvert, Bruce (1866–1940): born Jackson County; known as the Thoreau of Lake County; lived in a cottage near Griffith; published *The Open Road*, a philosophical magazine.

Carmichael, Hoagy (1899–1981): born Bloomington; songwriter; actor.

Christie, Dr. George T. (1881–1953): born Canada; professor at Purdue University.

Church, Ellen (1904–1965): the first airline stewardess; retired to Terre Haute.

Connelly, One-Eyed (dates unknown): noted gate-crasher who got into the 1926 Indianapolis 500-Mile Race without a ticket.

Corso, Lee (1935–): Indiana University football coach for ten seasons, beginning 1973.

Counsilman, James (Doc) (1920–2004): born Birmingham, Alabama; graduate of Ohio State University; swim coach at Indiana University, 1957–90; swam English Channel.

Craig, George N. (1909–1992): born Brazil, Indiana; Indiana governor, 1953–57.

Cuppy, William Jacob (1884–1949): born Auburn; critic; humorist; author; journalist.

D

Davis, Adelle (1904–1974): born Lizton; nutritionist and author.

Davis, Elmer H. (1890–1958): born Aurora; writer; radio journalist; during WWII was the director of the Office of War Information (OWI).

Dean, James (1931–1955): born Marion; actor.

Debs, Eugene V. (1855–1926): born Terre Haute; union leader; Socialist Party candidate for president; imprisoned for treason; released by President Warren Harding.

DeWitt, Joyce (1946–): born Wheeling, West Virginia; grew up in Speedway; actress.

Dillin, Samuel Hugh (1914–): born Petersburg; attorney; appointed federal judge, 1961.

Dillinger, John Herbert (1902–1934): born Indianapolis; moved to Mooresville; career as bank robber; shot outside a Chicago theater by FBI agents.

Douglas, Lloyd C. (1877–1951): born Columbia City; clergyman and novelist.

Dreiser, Theodore (1871–1945): born Terre Haute; writer and editor.

Dresser, Paul (1857–1906): born Terre Haute; songwriter; composer of "On the Banks of the Wabash, Far Away"; brother of Theodore Dreiser.

E

Eads, James B. (1820–1887): born Lawrenceburg; inventor and engineer; built bridges over the Mississippi River and jetties at its mouth.

Earhart, Amelia (1897–1937): born Atchison, Kansas; counselor at Purdue University; left from Purdue on the round-the-world flight on which she vanished in the Pacific.

Ehrmann, Max (1872–1945): born Terre Haute; attorney; poet, wrote "Desiderata" and several other volumes.

Ellsworth, Annie (1826–1918): born Lafayette; selected the first words to be sent over the telegraph by Samuel Morse on May 24, 1844.

Elmore, James Buchanan: (1857–1942): born near Alamo; known as the Bard of Alamo; sold his poems on the streets of Crawfordsville.

Erskine, Carl (1926–): born Anderson; National League pitcher with Brooklyn and Los Angeles Dodgers; became banker in Anderson.

F

Farmbrough, Ben (dates unknown): addressed a meeting at Boggstown, February 16, 1861, at which the town voted to join the Confederacy if the Union were to be divided.

Finley, Charles Oscar (Charley) (1918–1996): born Ensley, Alabama; moved to Gary at age two; worked and lived in La Porte; bought part of Kansas City Athletics and moved team to Oakland; created baseball's designated hitter.

Fisher, Carl Graham (1874–1939): born Greensburg; cofounded the Indianapolis Motor Speedway; developed Miami Beach.

Fisher, Jane (1894–1968): wife of Hoosier industrialist and entrepreneur Carl Fisher.

Flanner, Janet (pen name Genet) (1892–1978): born Indianapolis; lecturer; war correspondent; journalist writing from France.

Foster, John Watson (1836–1917): born Pike County; attorney; politician; diplomat; secretary of state, 1892–93.

French, Adam M. (dates unknown): one of the commissioners chosen to pick a name for the Boone County seat in 1832. The name Lebanon was selected either because of French's birthplace in Ohio or because the area reminded him of the cedars of Lebanon.

Frick, Ford (1895–1978): born Wawaka; DePauw University graduate; commissioner of baseball.

Fuller, E. Chubb (dates unknown): publisher of the *Agricultural Epitomist*, started in Indianapolis in 1881 and later moved to Spencer and called *Family Life.*

G

Gates, Ralph F. (1893–1978): born Columbia City; lawyer; Indiana governor, 1945–49.

Gatling, Richard Jordan (1818–1903): born Hertford County, North Carolina; lived in Indianapolis; invented the rapid-fire gun; sold two in the Civil War but after the war had a $175,000 order.

Gerard, Dave (1909–2003): born Crawfordsville; cartoonist, who drew Will-Yum, Citizen Smith, and other cartoons; mayor of Crawfordsville.

Gimbel, Bernard F. (1885–1966): born Vincennes; merchant; founded Gimbel's Department Store in New York City.

THE INDIANA BOOK OF QUOTES

Gresham, Walter Q. (1832–1895): born Lanesville; postmaster general; federal judge; secretary of the treasury under Chester Arthur; secretary of state under Grover Cleveland; presidential contender 1880 and 1892.

Grissom, Virgil I. (Gus) (1926–1967): born Mitchell; degree in mechanical engineering from Purdue University; joined Army Air Corps, 1944; one of the original seven Mercury astronauts; died in *Apollo 1* space capsule fire.

H

Hamilton, Lee H. (1931–): born Florida; moved to Evansville; graduate of DePauw University; winner of the Trester award in basketball; U.S. representative from Indiana.

Harper, Samuel Alain (1875–1962): born Orland in Steuben County; attorney; author.

Harris, Phil (1906–1995): born Linton; bandleader; actor; comedian.

Harrison, Benjamin (1833–1901): born North Bend, Ohio; came to Indianapolis to practice law; U.S. senator, 1881–87; twenty-third president, 1889–93.

Harrison, William Henry (1773–1841): born at Berkely, Virginia; governor of the Indiana Territory, 1801–13; elected ninth president, 1840; died after one month in office of pneumonia.

Harroun, Ray (1879–1968): born Spartansburg, Pennsylvania; winner of the first Indianapolis 500-Mile Race in 1911.

Hay, John Milton (1838–1905): born Salem; writer; statesman; ambassador; private secretary to President Abraham Lincoln; secretary of state.

Haynes, Elwood (1857–1925): born Portland; inventor; while living in Kokomo developed first car driven in the United States.

Hays, Will H. (1879–1954): born Sullivan; home Crawfordsville; lawyer and politician; postmaster general; president of Motion Picture Producers and Distributors of America.

Herold, Don (1889–1966): born Bloomfield; author of humor books; epigrammatist; wrote for newspapers and magazines; president of the Indiana University Alumni Association, 1943–45.

Hershey, Lewis B. (1893–1977): born near Angola; teacher; joined the Indiana National Guard in 1911; director of U.S. Selective Service.

Hesburgh, Theodore (1917–): born Syracuse, New York; graduate of Notre Dame University and its longtime president; ordained, 1943; member U.S. Civil Rights Commission.

Hodges, Gilbert Ray (Gil) (1924–1972): born Princeton; catcher, first baseman, outfielder; named to Baseball Hall of Fame, 1979.

Hoffa, Jimmy R. (1913–1975): born Brazil, Indiana; labor leader; believed murdered after disappearing July 30, 1975.

Hohenberger, Frank M. (1886–1963): born Ohio; lived in Indianapolis and Nashville, Indiana; photographer; columnist; author; known as the Sage of Brown County.

Howe, Edgar W. (1853–1937): born Treaty; author and journalist; editor of *Atchison (KS) Daily Globe.*

Hubbard, Frank McKinney (Kin) (1868–1930): born Bellefontaine, Ohio; hired by *Indianapolis News* in 1891 but left after three years; rejoined the *News* in 1901 and remained until his death.

Hulman, Anton Jr. (1901–1977): Terre Haute industrialist who purchased the Indianapolis Motor Speedway.

Humphreys, Robert E. (1870–?): born West Virginia; chemist; discovery of catalytic cracking at Whiting made development of automobile gasoline possible.

Hurty, John N. (1852–1925): born Lebanon, Ohio; first Indiana Health Commissioner; wrote the Indiana pure food and drug law of 1899 that served as the model for the federal act of 1906.

I

Indiana, Robert Clark (1928–): born New Castle; graduate of Arsenal Technical High School in Indianapolis; artist.

J

Jenner, William E. (1908–1985): born Marengo; U.S. senator from Indiana, 1947–59.

Jones, James Warren (Jim) (1931–1978): born Lynn; lived in Richmond; graduate of Butler University; pastor of the Peoples Temple; killed 913 followers in Guyana with cyanide in 1978.

Jordan, David Starr (1851–1931): born Gainesville, New York; student in Indiana colleges; professor at Butler and Indiana universities and other Indiana colleges; doctor and zoologist; author.

K

Karras, Alex (1935–): born Gary; football player; actor; sports announcer.

Kimbrough, Emily (1899–1989): born Muncie; lecturer; editor; scriptwriter; author; radio commentator.

Kinsey, Alfred (1894–1956): born Hoboken, New Jersey; joined Indiana University faculty in 1920 as assistant professor of zoology; researched and wrote *Sexual Behavior of the Human Male* and *Sexual Behavior of the Human Female.*

Kirkendall, Isaac (1787–1863): born Culpepper County, Virginia; candidate for sheriff in Kosciusko County, 1836.

Knight, Robert Montgomery (Bobby) (1940–): born Massillon, Ohio; basketball coach at Indiana University in Bloomington starting in 1971; firing in 2000 caused controversy.

L

Landgrebe, Earl F. (1916–1986): born Valparaiso; three-term congressman from Porter County.

Landis, Kenesaw Mountain (1866–1944): born Millville, Ohio; grew up in Indiana; jurist; first major league baseball commissioner.

Leahy, Frank (1908–1973): born O'Neill, Nebraska; graduate of University of Notre Dame; played football at Notre Dame and became its football coach in 1941.

Leonard, Bobby (1931–): born Terre Haute; attended Indiana University; played professional basketball with the Lakers and Chicago; coached the ABA Indiana Pacers.

Letterman, David (1947–): born Indianapolis; radio announcer; comic; host of late-night talk show.

Lilly, Eli (1885–1977): born Indianapolis; writer; head of pharmaceutical firm.

Lincoln, Abraham (1809–1865): born Kentucky; moved to Indiana in 1816; lived in Indiana until he was twenty-one years old; sixteenth president, 1861–65.

Little Turtle (Mishikinakwa) (ca. 1747–1812): Miami war chief.

Lombard, Carole (1908–1942): born Jane Alice Peters in Fort Wayne; moved to California, 1914; movie actress; first husband William Powell and second husband Clark Gable.

M

Main, Marjorie (1890–1975): born Mary Tomlinson in Acton; movie actress known for role as Ma Kettle.

Major, Charles (1856–1913): born Indianapolis; lived in Shelbyville; author.

Marshall, Thomas R. (1854–1925): born North Manchester; Indiana governor, 1909–13; vice president, 1913–21.

Martin, John Bartlow (1915–1987): born Hamilton, Ohio; to Indianapolis at age four; graduate of DePauw University; author; U.S. ambassador.

McCutcheon, John T. (1870–1949): born South Raub; reporter and cartoonist.

McGinnis, George (1951–): born Indianapolis; basketball player with Washington High School in Indianapolis, Indiana University, and ABA Indiana Pacers.

McQueen, Steve (1930–1980): born Indianapolis; raised Plainfield; actor.

Mellencamp, John Cougar (1951–): born Seymour; rock musician.

Miller, Casey (dates unknown): iceman at Crawfordville during Prohibition.

Miller, J. Irwin (1909–2004): born Columbus; attended Yale University; Columbus industrialist; political activist; philanthropist.

Miller, Joaquin (1839–1913): born Cincinatus Hiner Miller in Liberty; adventurer; lawyer; poet.

Morton, Oliver P. (1823–1877): born Salisbury; U.S senator; Indiana governor, 1861–67.

Muir, John (1838–1914): born Dunbar, Scotland; hurt in industrial accident; regained his sight in Indianapolis; left Indiana for California, where he became a renowned naturalist.

N

Nathan, George Jean (1882–1958): born Fort Wayne; author; editor; drama critic.

Nicholson, Meredith (1866–1947): born Crawfordsville; novelist; diplomat.

O

Owen, Robert (1771–1858): born Wales; socialist; philanthropist; founded utopian communities, including one at New Harmony.

P

Parseghian, Ara (1923–): University of Notre Dame football coach, 1964–74.

Peckham, Howard H. (1910–1995): born Michigan; historian; author; professor; director of the Indiana Historical Bureau and secretary of the Indiana Historical Society.

Perkins, Samuel E. (1811–1879): born Vermont; admitted to bar, Richmond; judge of the Indiana Supreme Court, 1844–64.

Poindexter, John (1936–): born Washington; admiral U.S. Navy; national security adviser, director, 1985–86.

Porter, Cole (1891–1964): born Peru; composer and lyricist.

Purdue, John (1802–1876): born Huntington County, Pennsylvania; located in Lafayette, 1839; philanthropist.

Pyle, Ernie (1900–1945): born Dana; reporter; author; killed by sniper in the South Pacific.

Q

Quayle, Danford (1947–): born Indianapolis; U.S. representative; U.S. senator; vice president, 1989–93.

Quayle, Marilyn (1949–): born Indianapolis; graduate of Purdue University and Indiana University law school; wife of Danford Quayle.

R

Reinisch, June Machover (1943–): born New York; professor at Rutgers University; director of the Kinsey Institute for Research in Sex, Gender, and Reproduction at Indiana University, 1982–93.

Reisner, George Andrew (1867–1942): born Indianapolis; professor; curator; Egyptologist; directed Egyptian expeditions.

Reynolds, Joseph (dates unknown): resident of Lafayette.

Riley, James Whitcomb (1849–1916): born Greenfield; journalist; poet.

Robertson, Oscar (1938–): born Charlotte, Tennessee; grew up in Indianapolis; played basketball with Crispus Attucks, University of Cincinnati, NBA Cincinnati Royals and Milwaukee Bucks.

Rockne, Knute (1888–1931): born Norway; played football at University of Notre Dame; football coach, 1918–31; died in plane crash.

Rose, Chauncey (1794–1877): came to Terre Haute in 1818; made fortune as a railroad builder; endowed school at Terre Haute named Rose Polytechnic Institute, later Rose-Hulman Institute.

Roush, Edd J. (1893–1988): born Oakland City; outfielder, mostly in the National League; inducted in the Baseball Hall of Fame, 1962.

Ruckelshaus, Jill (1937–): born Indianapolis; civil servant; lecturer; U.S. Civil Rights Commissioner.

Ruckelshaus, William D. (1932–): born Indianapolis; legislator; served terms as Indiana and U.S. deputy attorney general; officer with the United States Commission on Civil Rights; head of the Environmental Protection Agency (EPA).

S

Scholl, William M. (1882–1968): born La Porte; developed and manufactured foot products.

Schram, Emil (1893–1987): born Peru; president of the New York Stock Exchange, 1951–67.

Schroeder, William J. (1932–1986): Jasper resident; recipient of the world's first permanent artificial heart.

Scott, Blanche Stuart (1889–1970): born Rochester, New York; performed the first public flight by a female, October 1910, at Driving Park in Fort Wayne.

Shank, Samuel Lewis (Lew) (1872–1927): born Marion County; two-term mayor of Indianapolis (1910–13, 1922–26).

Shepherd, Jean (1921–1999): grew up in Hammond; scriptwriter; author.

Shoup, David M. (1904–1983): born Battle Ground; career marine; Medal of Honor, 1945; promoted brigadier general, 1953; commandant of Marine Corps, 1960; retired, 1963.

Shriner, Herb (1918–1970): born Toledo, Ohio; came to Fort Wayne when three years old; became known as the Hoosier Humorist.

Skelton, Red (1913–1997): born Vincennes; comedian on radio, stage, and screen; star of long-running television variety show.

Smith, Asa J. (1894–1973): born in Wabash; studied at DePauw University and Indiana Law School; pioneer attorney in Indianapolis; state representative.

Smith, Roy (dates unknown): officer with the Indiana Temperance League.

Smith, Walter Bedell (Beetle) (1895–1961): born Indianapolis; army officer; chief of staff to General Dwight D. Eisenhower; ambassador to the Soviet Union; undersecretary of state; author.

Soule, John L. B. (1815–1891): editor of the *Terre Haute Express.*

Stephenson, David Curtis (D. C.) (1891–1966): born Houston, Texas; came to Evansville in 1920; became grand dragon of the Ku Klux Klan in Indiana.

Stoff, Katy (dates unknown): tried on charges of keeping a tavern in Henry County in June 1867.

Stout, Rex (1886–1975): born Noblesville; author of detective fiction.

Stratton-Porter, Gene (1868–1924): born Wabash County; author and poet.

Sunday, William Ashley (Billy) (1862–1935): born Ames, Iowa; had home at Winona Lake (Kosciusko County) from 1914 until his death; evangelist.

T

Tarkington, Booth N. (1869–1946): born Indianapolis; author of numerous novels; served a term in the Indiana General Assembly.

Taylor, Marshall W. (Major) (1878–1932): born Marion County; noted black championship bicycle racer.

Tecumseh (1768–1813): born in Old Piqua, Ohio; Native American leader in the Northwest Territory.

Teetor, Ralph R. (1890–1982): born Hagerstown; inventor; industrialist; community leader; blinded in a childhood incident.

Terry, Edward (Tex) (1902–1985): born Coxville in Parke County; actor in B Western films.

Thacker, Tom (1939–): born Kentucky; basketball player with the ABA Indiana Pacers, 1969–70.

Tharp, Twyla (1941–): born Portland; dancer; choreographer.

Thomas, Isiah (1961–): born Chicago; basketball player Indiana University and NBA Detroit Pistons; coach of Indiana Pacers, 2000–2003.

Thomas, Kurt: (1956–): gymnast; Indiana State University NCAA championship team, 1977; U.S. Olympic team, 1976.

Thomas, Mary F. (1816–1888): born Maryland; first woman admitted to the American Medical Association; addressed the Indiana General Assembly pleading for female rights, January 6, 1859.

Toney, Ansel (1887–1987): lived in Farmland; became nationally known for making and flying kites.

Trueblood, David Elton (1900–1994): born Warren County, Iowa; Quaker professor at Earlham College starting in 1966; author of religious interpretations.

U

Urey, Harold C. (1893–1981): born Walkerton; chemist; professor; Nobel Prize, 1934.

V

Von Tilzer, Albert (1878–1956): born Indianapolis; followed in footsteps of his brother Harry and composed numerous hit songs, including "Take Me Out to the Ball Game."

Vonnegut, Kurt (1922–): born Indianapolis; novelist; lecturer.

Vukovich, Bill (1918–1955): born Alemeda, California; won the Indianapolis 500-Mile Race in 1953 and 1954.

W

Wakefield, Dan (1932–): born Indianapolis; writer; novelist.

Wallace, Lew (1827–1905): born Brookville; lawyer; army officer; author (*Ben-Hur*); territorial governor; minister to Turkey.

Wambsganss, Bill (1894–1985): born Cleveland, Ohio; came to Fort Wayne as toddler; attended schools and Concordia College there before "discovering" baseball; played in major leagues.

Ward, Mary Jane (1905–): born in Fairmount; author of *The Snake Pit* and other novels.

Watson, James E. (1864–1948): born Winchester; U.S. senator and U.S. representative from Indiana for twenty-nine years.

Wayne, Anthony (1745–1796): born Waynesboro, Pennsylvania; military officer; commanded troops in the Northwest Territory; Fort Wayne named in his honor.

Webb, Clifton (1889–1966): born Beech Grove; stage and film actor.

Weber, Dick (1929–2005): born Indianapolis; professional bowler; member of the American Bowling Congress Hall of Fame.

Wells, Herman B (1902–2000): born Jamestown in Boone County; president of Indiana University.

West, Jessamyn (1902–1984): born near North Vernon, Jennings County; novelist.

Wiley, Harvey W. (1844–1930): born Kent; chemist and food analyst; renowned for fighting against adulteration of food as chemist for the U.S. Department of Agriculture; instrumental in passage of the Pure Food and Drug Act of 1906.

Willkie, Wendell L. (1892–1944): born Elwood; business executive; lawyer; Republican presidential candidate, 1940.

Wooden, John (1910–): born Martinsville; basketball coach at the University of California at Los Angeles (UCLA); retired in 1975.

Woodfill, Samuel (1883–1951): born Jefferson County; sole Hoosier to win the Medal of Honor in World War I; called "America's greatest soldier" by General John J. Pershing.

Wright, Milton (1828–1917): born Rush County; minister; father of Wilbur and Orville Wright.

Wright, Orville (1871–1948): born Dayton, Ohio; joined brother, Wilbur, in bicycle shop; aircraft flights at Kitty Hawk.

Wright, Wilbur (1867–1912): born Millville near New Castle; flew at Kitty Hawk with brother Orville.

Z

Zoeller, Fuzzy (1951–): born New Albany; PGA golfer.

Index